THE 1976 PSYCHOLOGICAL ASSESSMENT OF TED BUNDY

THE 1976 PSYCHOLOGICAL ASSESSMENT OF TED BUNDY

Development of the Violent Mind

Book 4

AL CARLISLE, PHD

The 1976 Psychological Assessment of Ted Bundy

Al Carlisle, PhD

Book Four in the *Development of the Violent Mind* Series

Copyright © 2020 by Carlisle Legacy Books, LLC (2017 by Al Carlisle)

All rights reserved. No parts of this publication may be reproduced, stored in a retrieval system, or transmitted in any form or by any means, electronic, mechanical, photocopying, recording, or otherwise, without the prior written permission of the copyright owner, with the exception of short passages used in reviews.

The events described in this book are true, and many are part of public record. Some names and identifying details have been changed to protect the privacy of individuals involved.

ISBN: 978-1-952043-09-3

Library of Congress Control Number: 2020931128

Second Edition: January 2020 by Carlisle Legacy Books, LLC

First Edition: August 2017 by Genius Book Publishing

First edition edited by Leya Booth and Steven Booth

Second edition revised by Carrie Anne Keller, Dave Taylor, Steve Harmon, and C. Lindsay Carlisle

Cover designed by C. Lindsay Carlisle

Published by Carlisle Legacy Books, LLC
https://www.carlislelegacybooks.com

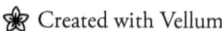 Created with Vellum

Contents

1. The 90-Day Diagnostic and Evaluation Unit — 1
2. The Psychology of the Crime — 9
3. What Is a Psychological Assessment? — 15
4. The TWIST Assessment — 21
5. Ted's Early Childhood — 29
6. Ted's Teenage Years — 43
7. Two Concerns — 49
8. College — 55
9. Marjorie and the University of Washington — 57
10. A Conversation with Sybil Ferris — 61
11. A Conversation with Marjorie — 69
12. Ted's First Trip to Philadelphia — 79
13. Liz Kendall and the Fall of 1969 — 85
14. Graduation from College and Seattle Harborview Hospital — 89
15. Kimberly — 93
16. Confirmation of Ted's Violent Personality — 99
17. Fall of 1972 — 105
18. Return of Marjorie — 109
19. Spring 1974. End of UPS — 117
20. The Salt Lake Period — 123
21. Getting Religious — 129
22. Thematic Apperception Test — 135
23. Putting it All Together — 151
24. Summary of the Findings — 157
25. Compartmentalization — 173
26. Aftermath — 179
27. Epilogue — 183

Appendix I	191
Appendix II	199
Appendix III	205
Appendix IV	213
Appendix V	225
Appendix VI	227
References	249
Acknowledgments	251
About the Author	255
Also by Al Carlisle, PhD	257
Publisher's Note	259

ONE

The 90-Day Diagnostic and Evaluation Unit

March 1976 holds a special significance for the course of my life. I was in my late 30s, working as a psychologist for the Utah Department of Corrections as part of a team of psychiatrists, psychologists, and social workers who were charged with evaluating convicted felons at the Utah State Prison in Draper, Utah, a small city south of Salt Lake. My office, in a large gray building on the east side of the prison, had a view of the beautiful Wasatch mountain range east of the prison. The mountain peaks still had snow on top, but soon they would be green and lush.

I had been working at the prison for several years and had assessed quite a number of offenders in that time. Few stand out in my mind today, over 40 years later, with one notable exception.

I checked my calendar that morning and saw that I only had one appointment scheduled with a new inmate who had just been committed to the 90-Day Evaluation Unit. I picked up his file and saw that the young man I was going to meet had been convicted of Aggravated Kidnapping, Felony I. I skimmed the file rather than reading deeply, as I did not want to bias my opinion of him before I had a chance to interview and test him. I glanced at his name as I went through Control One, the main security gate, and headed back into the main part of the prison. I could see at the other end of the corridor an inmate heading toward my office.

Theodore Robert Bundy.

Today, Ted Bundy is well known as perhaps one of the most famous and prolific serial killers in American history. Executed in Florida in January 1989, he has become an icon for romanticizing serial killers. Good looking, charming, and intelligent, Ted Bundy is often cited as the model for the kind of killer no one suspects. Indeed, Ted's friends, relatives, and co-workers stood by him adamantly during his arrests and trials. True crime author Ann Rule, who had known him when they both worked at a crisis hotline in Seattle, didn't initially believe that Ted was capable of the crimes that he had been accused of. She was not alone.

In the spring of 1976, the world knew practically nothing about Ted Bundy. Arrested in August, 1975 in Salt Lake City, Utah for "failure to stop at the command of a police officer," he was charged a few days later with "possession of burglary tools." Two months later, he was charged with the "aggravated kidnapping and attempted criminal homicide" of a young woman in Murray, Utah the previous November. On March 1, 1976, Judge Stewart M. Hanson, Jr. of the Third District Court in Salt Lake City found Ted guilty of the kidnapping charge. But because the case was largely circumstantial, and there were so many people standing up for Ted and insisting he was incapable of violence, Judge Hanson exercised his right to get an evaluation of Ted by the 90-Day team at the Utah State Prison. Our job: determine, to the best of our ability, whether Ted had the capacity for violence commensurate with the crime he had been convicted of.

I was the psychologist for the 90-Day Evaluation Program. It was my task to conduct psychological evaluations on inmates who were sent to the program by the court.

The process went like this: A person who had been found guilty of a crime by a judge or jury could be sentenced to time in prison or he could be put on probation. Occasionally, when a judge was uncertain how he wanted to sentence the offender, he could place the offender in the 90-Day Evaluation Program. While there, the offender would be evaluated by a committee consisting of a psychiatrist, a psychologist, and one or more social workers. Our reports would be given to the judge and he would use them in making a final determination of whether he would give the offender a "hard number"—a prison sentence—or grant probation.

In Ted Bundy's case, we were asked to give our opinions specifically about his potential for future violence.

When Ted approached me outside my office at the prison, he extended his hand and said, "Hi, I'm Ted Bundy. You must be Dr. Carlisle."

The man who stood before me was tall, good looking, and friendly. He wore an orange one-piece "jumpsuit" with the word DIAGNOSTIC stenciled on the back. He was smiling, cheerful, and confident, which I found to be a bit odd. Most offenders I worked with were hopeful rather than confident, especially considering that my opinion of them, along with the other team members on the Diagnostic Unit, could mean the difference between serving time in prison and receiving probation and treatment. But Ted approached me as if he already knew the outcome of my assessment—in his favor, of course—and his goal was to get to know the man who would return him to society when his 90 days had concluded.

Little did I know that my career and my life would never be the same after that moment.

Generally, the process we followed when evaluating an offender was straightforward and mostly routine. I would give him some psychological tests and I would interview him for a few hours. I would combine the test results and the interview findings and construct a report to present to the judge. And that would be it.

In Ted Bundy's case, the process was more complicated. The presenting question we on the committee were to address was whether we believed Bundy to be a violent person or would respond to treatment if put on probation.

Only a few criminals are sent to the prison diagnostic unit for psychiatric and psychological evaluations before a sentence is pronounced on them by the court. In Ted's case, there was a good reason for following this course. Ted was a student at the University of Utah Law School. He had been involved in political campaigns. He was intelligent, well dressed, and charming. There were people who claimed that the sheriff's office had arrested the wrong person and the court had incorrectly convicted Ted of a crime he didn't commit.

A Presentence Investigation Report had been conducted by Don Hull, an investigator for the Utah Department of Corrections Adult Probation and Parole Office. I had a copy of Mr. Hull's report. He had interviewed Bundy and had contacted friends and family to get their opinion of him. His report contained mixed findings about Ted.

I also had a copy of a psychological report by Evan Lewis, Ph.D. that had been submitted to the judge after the trial, which recommended to Judge Hansen that Ted be placed in the 90-Day program. It also had mixed results about Ted and, among other things, concluded that he wasn't fully open about himself. Dr. Lewis wrote in his report:

> Mr. Bundy... appears to be an intellectually bright man who is able to give socially acceptable responses to obvious questions, thereby disguising his true attitudes and beliefs. However, his background, his sometimes-inappropriate emotional reactivity, and his responses to more subjective measures belie his contention that he is a very emotionally stable and problem-free man.... Mr. Bundy is able to compartmentalize his emotions and thought processes to an unusual degree, possibly to the point that he can dissociate himself from one set of standards so that he can almost totally adapt another. Thus, he is probably capable of giving people very different impressions of himself, depending on what set of standards he chooses to guide his behavior. The test results uncovered no clear-cut reason as to why Mr. Bundy may have committed the crime of which he has been convicted, but some evidence of confusion and possibly hostility towards females was seen.

Dr. Lewis recommended that a more extensive evaluation be conducted at the Utah State Prison.

One disturbing factor was that Ted was suspected of killing several women in the State of Washington as well as in Utah and Colorado. However, despite intense investigations by multiple agencies in Washington, Ted had never been a suspect in any of them until two women disappeared from Lake Sammamish, east of Bellevue, Washington. A witness reported a man who approached one of the women to ask for help to load a boat on his car. She overheard him telling the woman that his name was "Ted." This witness said he drove a metallic colored Volkswagen. At that time, Ted owned a Volkswagen Beetle that matched that description.

This resulted in one of the largest manhunts ever to take place in the northwest. As the investigation progressed, Ted's girlfriend, Liz Kendall (her author name), had suggested to the police that Ted Bundy might possibly be the Ted they were looking for. She later retracted her statement but it was too late. The police were already considering him as a suspect. Since the police were starting to use computers to list and track names of potential suspects across jurisdictions for the first time in the history of criminal investigations, and finding Ted Bundy to be a name that had come up more than once, they began to look at him more closely.

My task as a psychologist on the team was to form my own opinion based on my independent findings and not be biased by what other investigators believed about him.

The best understanding of a person's personality and prediction about his future potential is often obtained from people who have known him in the past. Don Hull had talked to a number of people who knew Ted and had their phone numbers. To understand Ted, I decided that in addition to the routine psychological tests I would have him take as well as the interviews I would conduct with him, I would also talk to people who knew him to see if I could learn about Ted without being biased by Mr. Hull's report. If most of the people I spoke with told me that Ted was a good person, and that they detected no indications of violence within him, then I would accept that. However, if several people believed he was violent and if their stories were independent from each other, I would pursue the possibility that Ted did indeed have violent tendencies. Also, for my own satisfaction, if I concluded from the evidence that Ted *was* violent, I would have to find historical traces—actual evidence—that would tell me how he got that way and how he was able to be violent and yet able to hide it so well from others.

Surprisingly, Ted was open about me doing this. He even gave me the home phone number of his girlfriend, Liz Kendall. In addition, I was able to locate many people who had known him, some for years. I found them to be gracious in their willingness to talk to me about Ted.

I spent a great deal of time interviewing Ted and the people who knew him. When it came time for me to write my report, I felt that I had a reasonably complete picture of Ted's potential for violence.

This book is about how I came to understand Ted Bundy.

TWO

The Psychology of the Crime

One of the most important steps to approaching a psychological evaluation of an offender is to do a psychological analysis of the crime. I wanted to understand what kind of crime it was and what kind of person it would take to actually commit the crime the offender was accused of. That would give me a baseline for understanding the person himself.

An attempted kidnapping is a violent crime. Unless the offender is on drugs, is psychotic, or has something personal against the particular victim, the commission of a violent crime suggests that the origin of the violence may go deeper than this one act and may in fact be a chronic problem for the offender.

The Crime

Ted had been found guilty of attempting to kidnap a young woman, Carol DaRonch, from the parking lot outside Fashion Place Mall in Murray, Utah in the early evening of November 8, 1974.

Carol was walking into the mall when a man stopped her and asked if she owned the Camaro that was parked in the Sears section of the parking lot. She said she did. The man identified himself as a police officer. He said he thought somebody might have broken into her car and requested that she return to the parking lot with him to check her car to see if anything was missing, as well as to see if she could identify the thief if he was apprehended. Because the "police officer" was soft-spoken and well-dressed, Carol agreed to accompany him out to the parking lot.

When they arrived at her car, Carol looked inside and said she felt that nothing was out of place. He asked her to open the passenger door to check inside the vehicle, but she chose not to comply, since everything seemed to be where it was when she left it.

He then asked Carol to come with him to identify the burglar, who was being held in the parking lot on the other side of the mall. She again complied. When they arrived and the burglar was nowhere to be found, he announced that the burglar had been taken to a "Murray Police Substation." Carol followed him back through the mall, out to the parking lot, and then to a side maintenance door at the laundromat across the street from the mall, which was ostensibly the substation. It was locked. This suggests that he may have checked out the door prior to the crime. He told Carol it would be necessary to proceed to the main police station in his car.

On the way to his car, Carol asked him for some identification, at which time she was shown a "miniature size badge" that, for the moment, allayed her concerns.

Once inside his Volkswagen Beetle, Bundy made sure that Carol locked her door. He made a U-turn and headed to the vicinity of a school, where he pulled over, grabbed Carol, and tried to place a pair of handcuffs on her wrists. He succeeded in snapping them around her right wrist, but she fought him. He pulled out a pistol and told her that if she didn't stop resisting, he would shoot her. Instead of complying, Carol fought back even harder. The order of what happened next is in question, but according to Carol's witness statement, he threatened to strike Carol over the head with a long, heavy object like a crowbar. About the same time, Carol got the door open and escaped the Beetle. She ran out into the roadway and was picked up by a couple who admitted her into their car, and drove her to the police station. What happened to Bundy after that was unknown at that time.

This was not an impulsive, spur of the moment crime. It was planned. Bundy knew she had a Camaro. He knew where she had parked it and he had followed her from her car into the mall. However, the organization of his actions was somewhat deficient, suggesting a possible level of desperation in the mind of the offender. For example, he approached her in a busy mall where people walking by could have overheard at least part of the conversation. At one point before he approached her, she talked to a cousin in the mall. The offender identified himself as a police officer without clear identification and took her back out into the parking lot at a time when there were people walking and driving by. That's somewhat risky and suggests that the criminal was either in too much of a hurry or he was extremely confident in his ability to carry off the kidnapping without being detected.

Carol described the offender as well dressed, confident, and convincing enough that she didn't question his authority as a police officer.

This suggested that the offender likely had done this routine before and was confident that he would be successful. It suggested the offender may have kidnapped other victims.

Based on the evidence, a reasonable conclusion would be that the offender was intelligent. And perhaps the offender may have been desperate for one reason or another, so he wasn't as careful about some of the details as he might have been if he hadn't been in such a hurry.

The Arrest

Another issue to check on was Ted's story about the night he was arrested, Saturday, August 16th, 1975. He told me he had been restless that evening and went to see a friend who lived in the area of 21st South and 13th East in Salt Lake City, Utah. However, there was no proof that he had visited this person.

Ted claimed that, after midnight, he decided he wanted to go to the Kennecott Copper Mine (officially known as the Bingham Canyon Mine, one of the world's largest open-pit copper mines) because he thought they would be open all night. This didn't make sense because even if work was going on throughout the night, it wouldn't have been open to visitors.

He said that on his way out there he missed the turnoff so he started back home. Again, this doesn't sound totally logical. Had he missed the exit, all he would have had to do was to turn around and go back to the turnoff.

According to Ted, he pulled off into a housing area and stopped to smoke a marijuana joint at about 2:30 a.m. He saw a car coming around the corner and panicked. Ted said, "I just knew I wanted to get out of there." He threw the joint out the window and hurried off, driving through a stop sign. Ted said he was then pursued by a green car (even though it was a dark neighborhood) and he wasn't sure if it was a cop. He said the cops in Seattle have their police lights on top of their car and the car that was in back of him had a red light on the side of the car. Ted said he didn't know whether or not this was really a cop. He referred to the drive as "a typical neighborhood vigilante." Ted said he had forgotten to turn on his car lights. However, more accurately, he ran through multiple stop signs and was traveling at a high rate of speed. Ted was pulled over by Sergeant Robert A. Hayward of the Utah Highway Patrol. Sergeant Hayward asked him what he had been doing that evening. Ted replied that he had gone to a drive-in theater a short distance away—which of course was another contradiction. When the officer asked Ted the name of the movie, he gave the wrong answer.

The officer searched Ted's car and found a pair of handcuffs, which Bundy said he had purchased for his job as a security guard. Bundy also had strips of cloth and an ice pick, which he said were used for cleaning the runners of his car seat. The officer also found a crowbar, a mask, and some rope. Ted said the mask was an insert made out of pantyhose which he used under his ski mask to make it more comfortable.

His story didn't make sense to me. But still, it didn't prove that Ted was a violent person. It only suggested that Ted was caught smoking a joint and got spooked and tried to get away from the cop.

Ted's story about his reasons for driving around that late the night he was arrested sounded contrived. He was clearly caught off guard and was covering for something. He may have been an accomplished liar, but his inability to knit together a coherent alibi told me that he had not been expecting to get caught. This did not bode well for Ted. Innocent people don't expect to get "caught" either, but they tend to tell the truth about their circumstances and their alibis. Even if their stories sound farfetched, there is a certain internal logic to them, truth often being stranger than fiction. There was no internal logic to Ted's story. It was a jumble of unrelated facts strung together in an overtly contradictory fashion. Ted's poorly constructed story about his activities right before his arrest did nothing to help him avoid conviction. But it still didn't prove he was violent.

This was only the beginning of the assessment but, so far, the weight of evidence was against Ted.

THREE

What Is a Psychological Assessment?

A psychological assessment generally consists of a group of tests and interviews, often geared to answer specific questions such as the person's mental health and intellectual capabilities. There are various ways to do a psychological assessment and many reasons to do one. If a person is mentally ill, he may not be competent to cooperate in his own a. A person may have diminished intellectual capacity that needs to be taken into account when he is placed in prison where other inmates could take advantage of him. In the case of our program, if a person is believed through these assessments to be violent, then the judge can take that into consideration when determining options for punishment for a crime.

What A Psychological Assessment Can and Can't Tell You

Psychological assessments can tell you something about someone's personality, beliefs, emotions, and behavior. These tests are reasonably good at indicating whether a person has a problem with depression, anxiety, anger, or other issues like these. They can give you information about a person's capabilities. Psychological assessments are exceptionally good at determining the clarity of a person's thinking, which can be adversely affected by a number of factors, such as confusion from the use of mind-altering drugs or slowly progressing dementia.

Psychological tests only go so far. For example, it can tell you a person is depressed but it doesn't fully explain why he is depressed or how long he has been depressed, or give you the various factors that are causing the depression. Unless the subject is specifically asked—and indeed, answers honestly—a psychological assessment won't tell you what the person is planning to do about it.

A psychological assessment is a snapshot in time. It can tell you about the person as they are now, but not necessarily who they might become in the future. For example, a child who has been in and out of trouble for the first several years of his life may end up in prison, and some people will undoubtedly say, "See, I told you he was a trouble maker. I knew he would wind up in prison!" Another child with the same kind of background may turn it all around, graduate from college, and become highly successful in a career.

This kind of assessment is useful and accurate only to the degree to which a person is open and truthful. A psychiatric or psychological evaluation can tell you a person is psychotic with strong paranoid beliefs, but it won't tell you whether the patient will kill someone if you let him out of the hospital. The psychosis may clear up and stabilize on medications, but an assessment can't predict with certainty what will happen if he stops taking his medications.

By the same token, an evaluation can suggest that a subject has the capacity for violence, but not whether they will act on that potential. Research on this issue has tried to come up with a reliable way to predict future behavior but has not succeeded to the satisfaction of the scientific community.

Then Why Do an Evaluation on Ted Bundy?

What purpose would a judge have to send Ted for an evaluation at the prison? After all, he had been found guilty. Why not just give him a "hard number" (in other words, send him directly to prison to begin his sentence)? The answer is a bit complex.

When two girls disappeared from Lake Sammamish and a person who identified himself as Ted who drove a Volkswagen was named as the possible culprit, the police began searching for the suspect. A few people suggested that Ted Bundy might be their man. By that time, Ted had moved to Salt Lake to go to law school. The Salt Lake County Sheriff's Office received an alert about his presence in their jurisdiction.

When Ted was later arrested for attempting to abduct Carol DaRonch, there were a number of people who protested. They felt the authorities had arrested the wrong person. They were convinced that the Ted Bundy they were familiar with did not have the personality of a killer.

Richard Larsen, an Associate Editor of the Seattle Times, later wrote a book on Ted called *The Deliberate Stranger*, which was later made into a TV movie. Richard and his wife Virginia were in the courtroom when Ted was sentenced. Virginia told me that she felt so strongly that Ted was innocent that she was almost in tears when she heard Judge Stewart Hansen sentence him to prison.

Another person who believed Ted to be nonviolent was true-crime author Ann Rule, who worked at a crisis and suicide hotline with Ted for a period of time. As a crime writer, she was familiar with criminal personalities and investigations.

There's an important point to be made here. The people who spoke up for Ted were not naïve people who had only a cursory understanding of him. They were intelligent, well-educated, and successful in their professions. These people were not easily duped.

Was Ted the person they knew, a charming and easygoing man without the capacity for violence, or was Ted able to hide a dark side from most people, including his family and many of his close friends?

Was Ted a violent person or not? Judge Stewart Hansen was being fair in not jumping to conclusions that Ted was violent due to being found guilty of a single, isolated crime.

Approaching the Evaluation

What we faced as evaluators in the 90-Day Evaluation Program was a seemingly successful student and aspiring politician who came to Salt Lake to work on a law degree. At the time of my evaluation of Ted, I was aware of that he was a potential suspect in homicides in Washington before coming to Utah, but because he had not been convicted of any of these crimes, I was unable to use any of that as evidence of violence.

Debby Kent went missing a few hours after the attempted abduction of Carol DaRonch. The description people gave to the police fit Ted. But again, there was no proof that he was the one who had abducted her. These were all suppositions without proof, and I couldn't use any of them in drawing my conclusions.

Dr. Lewis had previously concluded that Ted had the potential for violence, though the findings were mixed. The only thing Dr. Lewis could conclude with certainty was that

Ted was untruthful in his answers to the assessments. The Presentence Evaluation written by Don Hull had some significance because Don obtained firsthand information from people who knew Ted.

Unfortunately, I couldn't use his reports as evidence of Ted's potential for violence either. I had to start from the beginning.

FOUR

The TWIST Assessment

(TWO WORD INCOMPLETE SENTENCES TEST)

Personality and IQ tests are part of a battery of tests that can be used in a psychological assessment. I administered several of these tests to Ted. He scored in the Superior range on an IQ test I gave him, which I could have predicted. After speaking with him for a short time, I could see he was intelligent.

He was given a personality test that asks a person to read a sentence and then mark the sentence either true or false as he sees himself. The test measures levels of anger, depression, and anxiety as well as other emotional and personality factors.

Ted scored very low on each of these dimensions, meaning he did not have any of the personality traits being assessed. By scoring low, he was telling me that he had none of these problems. This is not an easy achievement because the test is designed to cross-reference different dimensions of one's personality, thus making the test hard to fool. His results were not entirely surprising, however, because he had previously been given the Minnesota Multiphasic Personality Inventory (MMPI), a similar true-false personality test where he had scored low on all of the scales, which would indicate no presence of an emotional problem. This didn't seem accurate, however, because a person who is, or may be, spending a lot of time in prison just doesn't score this low in all of these areas. Either Ted was telling the truth and he was trouble-free, or he was exceptionally good at lying about it.

When Ted's scores didn't match the normal profile of a convicted felon facing prison time, it made the evaluation much harder. I had no choice but to conclude that something was wrong and that Ted was working hard—and well—to hide something. The personality test couldn't indicate what he was hiding. I had to dig deeper.

Another test I gave Ted was the Two Word Incomplete Sentences Test (TWIST), a sentence completion test created by Dr. Allan Roe of Psychological Resources, Inc. This test consists of 38 beginnings of sentences of varying length, and the subject is asked to finish each sentence using one or two words only. This is a projective test in which a person says things about his personality without always being fully aware of just what he is saying about himself, and is thus harder to fool. For the most part, if a person taking this test does not want to appear violent, he will obviously not give an answer such as:

I consider myself to be a… "violent person."

On the other hand, even if the subject of the test is trying hard to conceal a personality problem, the likelihood is that he will write some answers that hint at the truth. The value of this test is not only in the individual answers themselves, but in the pattern across answers, which reflects the person's thoughts and concerns beyond what a single answer will give.

When a person finishes the sentences in a sentence completion test, there may be multiple levels of meaning representing multiple levels of awareness or consciousness within the person. The first level may be an answer given to comply with the demands of the evaluation but also one designed to avoid revealing himself. However, there is sometimes a deeper, more hidden meaning. I have no doubt that when Ted took the TWIST, he attempted to write his answers in a way that would keep me from observing anything that would suggest anger or violence. He wanted to make a good impression for the court. Naturally, this is to be expected. If an offender is taking a psychological assessment that could possibly make the difference between leniency and harsh punishment, he will take whatever approach that seems most logical in order to achieve this outcome.

The following is Ted's sentence completion items on this test, administered on April 1, 1976 at the Utah State Prison. The spelling is his. He printed his answers in capital letters. (Please note, Ted didn't follow the instructions to answer with only two words. In fact, it is common for the subject of this test to overlook that instruction.)

1. I feel: "CHALLENGED."
2. My mind is: "ACTIVE."
3. A good way to relax is: "TO LISTEN TO MUSIC."
4. A person just isn't himself when: "AFFRAID."
5. It would be too easy to: "BE DEPRESSED."
6. It's hard to express feelings of: "PRISON LIFE."
7. The only thing that really matters in this world is: "HAPPINESS AND PEACE."
8. Things would be great if I could: "BE AQUITTED."

9. I've never: "HURT ANYONE."
10 I need: "FREEDOM."
11 I feel I have to: "KEEP LEARNING."
12. A person is most helpless when: "WITHDRAWS FROM OTHERS."
13. My mother was usually: "LOVING."
14. Most people think I am: "(WHO KNOW ME) INNOCENT."
15. Marriage is: "INTIMATE PARTNERSHIP."
16. I can't: "STOP STRUGGLING."
17. I wish I hadn't: "COME TO UTAH."
18. It's easy to get into trouble when: "OTHERS AREN'T CONSIDERED."
19. When I was a child I felt: "CONSTANT ADVENTURE."
20. I want to know why: "ABOUT EVERYTHING."
21. I am: "CONFIDENT."
22. Drugs are: "DESTRUCTIVE."
23. Worse than being lonely is being: "UNLOVED."
24. Women are: "MEN'S EQUALS."
25. I hate: "PREJUDICE."
26. When frustrated I: "I DESENSITIZE."
27. The thing I remember about my father was: "BOUNDLESS ENERGY."
28. In the future there will be: "NEW OPPORTINITIES."
29. Compared to most families mine usually: "WAS CLOSE."
30. What excites me is: "SPRING-TIME."
31. I don't like people who are: "SOLICITOUS."
32. I think most girls should: "BE THEMSELVES."
33. My greatest weakness is: "PROCRASTINATION."
34. Someday I will become: "AN ATTORNEY."

35. I wish I could lose the fear of: "HYPERDERMIC NEEDLES."
36. I was proud of myself when: "FINISHED COLLEGE."
37. I couldn't live without: "CARING PEOPLE."
38. Tests like this are: "OBLIGATORY; OBTUSE."
(Editor's Note: Appendix V contains an image of the actual test response sheet filled out by Ted.)

Analysis

According to the assessment, Ted felt challenged (item 1) about what the court's final conclusions might be regarding him doing time in prison. It would be easy to be depressed about it (item 5). However, he needed his active intelligent mind (item 2) to be free from distractions if he was going to devise solutions to the obstacles facing him. If he allowed himself to feel much fear (item 4), it might diminish his mental capability to be successful in facing his challenges. However, it won't be easy and he can't stop struggling (item 16) even though he feels confident (item 21).

So, how does Ted handle the situation when he feels it might not turn out well for him? How does he keep himself from being controlled by the normal fear and anxiety that most people would feel if they were in his shoes? He desensitizes (item 26). It's a technique he likely learned in one of the psychology classes he took in college.

Desensitization is a psychological process used to help a person reduce a fear that is controlling him. It's commonly used to get rid of a fear of snakes, or of flying, or of having a panic attack when around crowds.

At first, I didn't catch on to what Ted meant by desensitizing. A few days later when I was interviewing him about his history, I asked him if there was anything he was afraid of. He suddenly had an angry look on his face, his voice was loud, and he looked into my eyes and said,

> "I don't have fears! Fear, pain, and punishment don't stick with me!"

It wasn't the words that stood out, it was the intensity of the anger in his voice. It appeared that he viewed fear as a weakness and was determined that he would have none of it. It appeared that Ted might have applied the process of desensitizing to get rid of fear (and possibly guilt).

There were other items in the sentence completion test that seemed to have meaning as well. Sometimes a person will carry a thought from one item to the next. Items 6 to 11 appear to possibly share a common thought.

He had difficulty with prison (item 6). It would be an extension of his jail time, but even worse. He desperately needed happiness and peace (item 7). This is particularly important because the beginning of the sentence is, "The *only* thing that really matters in this world is…" In spite of him attempting to convince me (and probably himself) that fear, pain, and punishment didn't stick with him, he couldn't find peace.

He hoped to be acquitted (item 8). He wanted to tell me he had never hurt anyone (item 9) and he needed freedom (item 10). And, in order to get what he was after in life, he had to keep learning (item 11).

Item 12 is particularly interesting. He is saying that a person is *most* helpless when he withdraws from others. This seems to be a repetition in meaning to item 4. A person withdraws from others when he is depressed or afraid. Ted seemed to be saying that when he withdrew from the association and support of others, he was most helpless.

Item 18 is also interesting. It's easy to get into trouble when "others aren't considered." This item appears to have multiple meanings. From what I saw, Ted was lonely when he was young. This suggests that maybe he wasn't "considered" or loved as much as he wanted or needed. If this is accurate it could have resulted in him getting involved in inappropriate things. Also, if he did kill the girls the police were beginning to blame him for, it would be because he didn't consider their lives to be important. This would suggest self-centered thinking.

Item 23 is an extension of items 7, 37, and 16. He is saying (item 23) that he is fearful of not being loved. Perhaps he didn't feel loved when he was growing up. Or perhaps he might have been seriously hurt when a particular girl (or girls in general) that he loved didn't love him back. He can't find the "happiness and peace" he requires (item 7) unless he has "caring people" (item 37). This may be *part* of the reason he can't "stop struggling" (item 16). There is also a contradiction between this item saying he can't stop struggling and his statement that he doesn't have any fears.

The findings from the TWIST say something about Ted's personality and could give collateral support to the conclusion that Ted is violent. Still, nothing here indicated clearly that he was.

I had to look elsewhere for answers.

FIVE

Ted's Early Childhood

When doing a psychological assessment, I always get a detailed history of the offender's life. If I am going to tell the court Ted is a violent person, I have to justify my conclusions based on a combination of test and interview results including the person's history. If Ted is violent, developmental facts from his past will often explain how he got that way.

Ted answered my questions easily and seemed to have no difficulty mobilizing his intellectual abilities during our interview. His answers were quick, short, and to the point.

Ted was born to Louise Cowell at the Elizabeth Lund Home for Unwed Mothers in Burlington, Vermont on November 24, 1946. He said,

> My mother was involved in activities in school and she was at the top of her class. She was intelligent, active, and outgoing. She was on the yearbook staff. She became pregnant with me shortly after she grad-

uated. She could have gone on to college but she didn't have a scholarship.

I was aware that he was illegitimate and I assumed that this might be an issue with him. World War II had ended a year prior to Ted's birth and people were attempting to get their lives back together again. Being an illegitimate child in 1946 was a disgrace to his mother and a humiliation to the entire family. His mother had to go out of state to have her first child. An abortion was unthinkable.

When I later asked him about it, he said his illegitimacy had no effect on him. I didn't want to argue the point, and there are often good reasons for not mentioning one's illegitimacy, so I decided not to pursue this issue at this time. If his illegitimacy *was* an issue, it would likely come up again without me having to bring it up. He said he "moved" to Philadelphia from Vermont. He didn't mention that he was born in a home for unwed mothers.

Ted said he never knew of his father, but he "had a strong curiosity about him." He said he initially lived in a large house with his mother, grandparents, and aunts, and that he received a lot of attention from his two teenage aunts.

> They were like my sisters when I was a little kid. They fussed over me. My grandparents doted over me because I was their first grandchild.

This was an interesting statement. He didn't say anything about any attention or caring he received from his mother. The attention came from his aunts.

This was a curious statement, and I wasn't quite sure what he meant by that. It had been reported to me that Ted was led to believe his mother was his sister and his grandparents were his parents. Ted denied this but if this was true it would pose a problem when he moved to the northwest with his "sister" rather than remain in Philadelphia with his "parents."

Ted was four years old when he and his mother moved to Tacoma, Washington where other relatives lived. As to what Tacoma was like for him, he said,

> It was a time of readjustment. Life was not as sweet but it wasn't a nightmare. Life centered around mom. It didn't have the completeness it had. It was a smaller world.

This type of statement from Ted was common throughout the interview. He would say something negative ("Life was not as sweet...") then attempt to undo it as if to make sure I didn't get the wrong impression ("...but it wasn't a nightmare."), then he would return to the negative statement ("It didn't have the completeness it had.").

In Tacoma, his mother got a job as a secretary at the Methodist Council of Churches and met and later married John Culpepper Bundy, a military veteran who was working as a dietician at the VA hospital at Fort Lewis, Washington. Regarding the reason for the move, Ted said,

> It was possibly for mother to start over again. Both
> mother and grandfather were strong-minded people.

Does that mean that Louise and her father didn't get along? It had been mentioned in another report that Louise's father had a temper. Did Ted's mother move to the northwest to get away from her family? Ted was originally named Theodore Robert Cowell. His mother legally changed his name to Nelson in a Philadelphia court before moving to Tacoma. Was this to make it easier to hide his illegitimacy? She was moving to live with her brother, John "Jack" Cowell, and it could raise questions if Ted's name was also Cowell.

Ted was five years old when his mother married John Bundy. They moved to the country.

> Dad had a small house. We had pigs and chickens
> and things were fine again. I had a dog named Lassie.
> We were in a sparsely populated area.

"…and things were fine again"? This suggests that things weren't so fine at first. Louise's brother Jack lived in Tacoma and was a professor of music at the University of Puget Sound. Ted was fond of his aunt and uncle but his relationship with their son, his cousin John Jr., was another matter.

> Aunt Eleanor came from a wealthy family—the
> upper crust. Uncle Jack didn't have many things.
> Aunt Eleanor was frail and had breakfast in bed. She

was very intelligent and I felt close to her. She was
very refined. She never shouted, and was restrained.

This says volumes about his aunt's family, and perhaps about their personalities. He admired his Aunt Eleanor because she was intelligent and refined. She came from wealth which was a strong contrast to the relatively poor circumstances in Ted's family. When Ted went to college, he attempted to appear intelligent and refined, which I learned from telephone conversations I had with people acquainted with him.

Ted said positive things about his Uncle Jack. He admired the fact that Jack was a professor of music at the University and, perhaps because of his association with Uncle Jack, Ted liked classical music. He had also said good things about Aunt Eleanor. He had mentioned his aunts who spoiled him when he was in Philadelphia, and even discussed his grandfather, who took the role of a father. But so far, he had said nothing about his mother.

Ted and his cousin John were close to the same age and there was a competitive relationship between them. Speaking of John, Ted said,

My cousin saw me as a spoiled brat. He was bigger and stronger and beat me in wrestling. Aunt Eleanor wanted John to have a mansion and a Rolls Royce. I envied John when he said he planned on going to school in Paris. However, I had a good relationship with John later on, and we were like brothers.

So far there have been a few significant themes mentioned which may have had an effect on the development of Ted's personality:

- Wealth contrasted with poverty (or Ted's perception of poverty).
- Cousin John was likely to inherit wealth, whereas Ted was not.
- Competition with a cousin over wealth and physical strength.
- Admiration of his uncle who was a music professor in college.
- Admiration of his aunt who was refined but frail.

Ted reported that he was close to his mother when he was young but he had little respect for his stepfather. As other children came into the home, he was in the difficult position of being the oldest child, yet a stepson. He had lost the emotional contact with his grandparents and now he was required to share his mother with a stepfather and younger half-siblings. He had a sister Linda born in 1952, a brother Glenn in 1954, followed by another sister Sandra in 1956, and then another brother Richard in 1961. He was closest to Richard.

His life at that time consisted of family, school, and association with kids in his neighborhood. He enjoyed spending evenings outside talking to neighborhood friends. He wasn't abused by his parents and he and others described his parents as God-fearing people. He was raised in a conservative religious family with a strong work ethic. Ted was also active in his church.

. . .

In the middle of our conversation about his childhood, the topic shifted to Ted's later work at the Crisis Clinic in Seattle, while he was going to college. He said, "It did wonders for my life."

This statement about the crisis clinic came as a bit of a surprise. It was out of context. I took it to mean Ted was insinuating that his cousin John was born with a silver spoon in his mouth while Ted had to earn everything he achieved. I asked if the issues with his cousin John had any effect on his life. He said, "I can't see any." As to the people he looked up to when was a child he said,

> Grandfather [in Philadelphia] had an intense interest in literature and science. He could martial his resources. He overpaid his workers and undercharged his customers. I [also] admired Uncle Jack and I patterned my life after him. He was thoughtful and well educated. He was always warm and he knew about life.

Again, he didn't mention his mother or his stepfather, John Bundy, as role models in his life. Sometime before Ted began kindergarten, roughly around his fifth year, he and his family moved to Browns Point, Washington:

> There were not a lot of other kids there. I had one friend a half a mile away and another a couple of miles away. We had a lot of fun together. We were like the Three Musketeers.

I asked him if he was lonely as a child. He said, "Maybe I was a little lonely but it was not pervasive."

After living about a year in Browns Point the family moved back to Tacoma in time for Ted to start kindergarten. He spent kindergarten, 1st, and 2nd grade at the Sherman Elementary School.

> We were in a Catholic and an Italian neighborhood and I was neither Catholic nor Italian. The Italians seemed fierce and I ran away from them to avoid getting hurt.

The first grade was,

> …not eventful. The teacher got pregnant and the substitute teacher was big and she had a scowl but I learned to love her.

About his second-grade teacher he said,

> She was an orthodox Catholic. She was firm and when she came to class, she asked who had been to Catechism. She put the fear of God in you.

She got after Ted on one occasion. He was playing marbles with another boy. They got into an argument. Ted hit the kid ("I only hit him twice"). Apparently, this transgression was more than the teacher was willing to abide, and she punished Ted. He said this teacher was one of the worst he had because her discipline was arbitrary.

Following the 2nd grade the family moved to a newer area of Tacoma. The schools and neighborhoods and recreation areas were closer, and more kids lived near him. There were undeveloped wooded areas close by. Ted lived "in a small box house" until he graduated from high school. In the early 1950s, Ted listened to the weekly serials on the radio.

> I wished Roy Rogers would adopt me. My life was boring and the life of Roy Rogers was more exciting.

He reported nothing particular about the 3rd grade. He had Mrs. Ryan in the 4th grade.

> She was a voluptuous disciplinarian but she treated me well. She took an interest in me. She was pleasant.

She was a disciplinarian but was she was viewed as pleasant because she took an interest in Ted? This was the first time Ted said anything about anyone taking an interest in him since he moved back to Tacoma.

Additionally, I began to wonder about his observation that Mrs. Ryan was "voluptuous." This statement was coming from a 30-year-old man, not a 4th grader, but it is uncommon for people to attribute sexual concepts to adults they knew as children. This was worth filing away.

At this point, Ted said something about his 4th grade experience that was very personal. It was about his reading ability.

> I longed to be in the inner circle but I was average. I was envious of the kids at the top reading level and it humiliated me that I wasn't up there with them.

Up to this point in the interview Ted had made several negative statements about his life and the people involved in it, but each time he tried to reverse the negative impression he was making. This time he didn't.

His previous statements were about his living conditions. This statement about reading was the first he made that would suggest the degree to which he might have been affected by what was happening in his life.

He said that there were kids from "Pill Hill" in his class in school. These were kids from wealthy families who had swimming pools. Ted's family was poor. Was Ted so needy in his desire to achieve wealth like his relatives that he was "humiliated" because he was not at the top reading level in class? The term "humiliated" was a strong word to use in this situation, particularly for a boy who is only in the 4th grade.

In the 5th grade, Ted had a teacher who was from Germany.

> She was very competent; she was more of a teacher and less a caretaker and keeper of discipline. I developed an interest in politics through the history studies. I improved in reading and academics went well.

This suggested that when Ted was in a class in which he was happier he was able to put more thought towards his interests. I was intrigued that he developed a desire to study politics and history at this age. This is quite unusual for a 5th grade student and it likely reflected his innate intelligence.

He had a Mr. Josies in the 6th grade. Ted said Mr. Josies took an interest in him. Once more Ted seemed to feel he could develop some of his interests without fear of criticism. He said he felt more confident in his abilities and he started playing football.

The 7th, 8th, and 9th grades were more enjoyable. He got B's in his classes and he spoke of his teachers in affectionate terms. He hadn't yet developed goals for his future. He ran for student body vice president and said he lost a close race. He ran hurdles in track and took third place but said, "I wasn't the greatest runner." He played on the football team as a split end or halfback. He was active in school and sports and just missed getting on the basketball team.

When I asked him what his personality was like in junior high, he said,

> It's hard to say. I had a lot of friends but I became less dependent on friends and I was more of an individualist. I was interested in things that were going on around the country. I memorized things I heard on the radio. I was less interested in peers and more of an individual.

This didn't make sense to me. Socializing is very important to a boy during these years. If he was less interested in friends why would it be so important for him to be on the football and basketball teams and to run for a political position in school? Ted had been concerned about fitting in but now he was suggesting that this was no longer the case. Earlier he had talked about the time he had two close friends; they called themselves the Three Musketeers. He spoke of that relationship in glowing terms. Now he was saying that friends were less important.

Around this time, I made a phone call to a woman (Mrs. W) who lived in Ted Bundy's neighborhood had had known him and his family.

A: When did you know Ted?
W: I knew him in junior high and high school.
A: What was he like then?
W: He seemed like a levelheaded guy. A bunch of us would get together and we would sit on one of the kid's porches in the evenings and talk.
A: Did you see any change in his personality between junior high and high school?
W: No. However, in high school he never really did things with girls. He had a lot of friends [it turned out, in fact, that he only had two actual friends, the rest being "friendly acquaintances"] but didn't get involved with social activities. I don't recall him having any girlfriends in school.
A: What was his personality like?
W: Well, in certain things he was outgoing but in others he was shy. With people he knew, he was more outgoing, but with people whom he didn't know he

wasn't all that outgoing. I don't recall the kids picking on him. He was a highly intelligent kid.

A: How was his relationship with his family?

W: There was no problem that I could see. He was busy and he always seemed to be doing things around the house. I remember him going to basketball and football games but I don't remember him going to dances.

A: Were you aware of any personal problems he might have had?

W: No, I don't remember him having any personal problems.

A: Overall, what was your impression of him?

W: I always had a relatively good impression of him. It wasn't a great impression but it wasn't negative. He was a friendly person but he didn't seem to stand out in any way.

The information I had gathered through this part of our interview raised some important points. For example, Mrs. W remembered him as friendly, somewhat shy, and intelligent, but there was nothing particularly noteworthy about him. From Ted and other sources, I had learned that there were no indications of physical or sexual abuse in the home. He had a good, though not terribly close, relationship with his mother but not so much with his stepfather. He was clearly competitive in school, having tried out and made the football team, and just missed getting on the basketball team, but he didn't report any confidence-building successes as a child. Did his statement about having less interest in social relationships as he approached his teenage years suggest that something might have gone wrong and that he was withdrawing?

At this point in the interview there were several issues of interest that I hadn't resolved:

- What did he believe about his biological father?
- What affect did his mother getting married to John Bundy and then having other children have on him?
- What affect did the wealth of his Aunt Eleanor have on him since Ted's family was poor?
- What affect did his cousin John have on him? When John spoke of his future possibilities of greatness because of having wealth, how did that affect Ted?
- Why would Ted relate negative experiences and then deny they had any effect on him?
- When he was young, the radio was the primary means for a child to hear adventure stories. Ted listened to the weekly serials that were common then. As with many of us at that age, we would develop fantasies about being the hero in the story. However, it was uncommon for a child to listen to political speeches and even more so to memorize parts of them. Why was Ted so interested in them?
- Why was Ted not more open about himself?

SIX

Ted's Teenage Years

It was easy to talk to Ted. He was friendly, he smiled a lot, he didn't seem overly tense, and he talked freely. The Ted Bundy who sat across the desk from me spoke more as a friend than as a violent criminal who was possibly going to lose his career, his reputation, and may have to spend several years in prison for attempting to kidnap and possibly kill a woman. I could see why many people refused to believe that he was guilty of his given crime.

Since I first evaluated Ted in 1976, I have studied him in more complete detail than I had the time for then. Ted is possibly the most studied serial killer in history and many writers have given accounts of his childhood. They have reported neglect (his mother Louise leaving him in the unwed mother's home for three months because she didn't want to accept him), fear of and abuse from a violent grandfather, and Ted inserting knives into an aunt's bed in Philadelphia when he was three years old. While any or all of these things might be true, I didn't have any confirmation of that information when I did my evaluation for the court. Stories misremembered by sincere people (let alone deliberate false information inserted into history by attention seekers) are commonly found when attempting to explain violence. If Ted was violent, I wanted to be able to trace the logical development of it through the years. I didn't want to jump to any conclusions and risk misunderstanding Ted.

At this point in the interview we had covered his elementary school years. Personality problems that begin in early childhood often begin to show themselves during the teen years. The next section of our interview was about his junior high and beginning high school years. In particular, I wanted to know if he went on any dates. He said,

> I dated some girls in junior high. I went to parties with the socially adept.

This is interesting. He had previously indicated that he was becoming less interested in social activities and yet he states here that he went to parties with the "socially adept." Did Ted not consider himself to be among the "socially adept?" There may be something missing here.

> *Did you kiss any girls?*
> Yeah.
> *Did you engage in any sexual touching with girls?*
> Uh huh. Yeah, I did.
> *Well Ted, what happened? I understand you didn't go on any dates during high school. You went to a dance with a girl in the 12th grade but that was about it. It appears*

there was a change in your personality. You began dating and you had an interest in girls including kissing and getting sexually involved but then you stopped. What happened?
[Pause.] Well, gee Al, I don't know what it could have been.

This again suggested there was something he wasn't telling me. There were possibly two things of importance here. First, he said he didn't know the answer as to why he stopped associating with girls. He had said he was becoming more of an individualist and less interested in social activities. He starts engaging in sexual activities with girls, but then all of this shuts down and he doesn't have anything to do with girls until his senior year in high school. It's almost inconceivable that he couldn't give an explanation for it or that he hadn't ever considered the question. Most people in his position would at least have tried to explain this sort of thing, even if only to themselves.

Second, through the entire interview, Ted had quick and logical answers to my questions. There were times, however, when I asked a question that seemed to catch him off guard. At such time, he would be more hesitant to give an answer. It was his hesitancy in answering the question that was sometimes as important as the answer he would give.

I asked him what the 10th grade was like for him.

I can't remember very much about it. I was not a whiz in French but I enjoyed English.

What was your social life like?
It revolved around the same group I had been associating with up to that time. I didn't adapt to the broader social schemes. I restricted myself to my friends in the neighborhood. At times I felt left out as my friends went off in other directions.
What kept you from going in other directions in your life as some of your friends were doing?
I felt apprehension towards establishing new relationships. I was just as secure with academic life. Social relations were not important to me.
What was the 11th grade like for you?
I didn't join any groups. I didn't turn out for football or other sports. I had no drive to get into clubs. I felt school was principally going to class and doing well in my classes.
Why didn't you go on any dates?
My mother was able to pay the bills for the home but there wasn't a lot of money. I had to earn my own spending money.
How did you do it?
I had a lawn cutting business. We didn't get any money for doing chores around the house.

There are several contradictions here relative to what Ted had indicated earlier and what he would say later. He had no drive to get into clubs or sports during high school. He didn't branch out socially. He didn't go on dates, and his explanation of not having money was plausible but not terribly satisfying. The question became, why was he turning inward rather than outward like his peers? This is not typical adolescent behavior, and required a more complete explanation.

Ted had pursued relationships with girls at the beginning of his junior high years and would later attempt to join a fraternity in college. What happened during high school?

> *How were things with your father?*
> He was extremely busy digging, gardening, rebuilding. He couldn't sit down. The primary contact with my father was him directing and telling me things I should be doing. I was closer to my mother.
> *How about the 12th grade? What was it like?*
> I did well in school. I helped others run for student body offices when I was in the 11th grade and it helped with my social life in the 12th grade. I looked forward to going to college and getting a scholarship to Puget Sound. I felt my social deficits were cured.

Again, an emphasis on his social life. It was clearly a sore spot for him, or he wouldn't keep focusing on it. But other questions were raised. What were his social deficits? How were they cured? Why was he dodging around the social relationship issue? Why didn't he just come out and tell me why he was shy or something simple like that?

> *But you only went to one or two dances. Why not more?*
> I had neutral feelings about girls. There was no inhibitions or fear, just a lack of motivation. I didn't have a car at that time. When I got out of school, I got a lucrative job which allowed me to get my first car, a 1933 Plymouth Coup. I was becoming an individual.
> *Did you have any goals for the future?*

> I wanted to graduate from college, find a beautiful coed and work for the government.

Ted had neutral feelings and a lack of motivation regarding girls? And yet his goal for the future was to find a beautiful coed? If he wasn't interested in girls for the purposes of sex and romance, why the emphasis on finding a beautiful coed?

During the 11th grade, he helped some of his friends run for student body offices. This opened up an avenue for him to become included in their activities which, it was becoming clear, was something he didn't otherwise have access to. That must have been frustrating and depressing for him.

In the 12th grade, and possibly during the 11th grade as well, he went skiing with friends and acquaintances on weekends. This was his main social activity at the time. He devised a way to forge counterfeit ski tickets so he and his friends would be able to save money when they went skiing. He bleached off letters from the old tickets and used a rubber stamp and colored stamp pads to create new ones. He was proud of this. That raised the question, was he proud of other aberrant behavior? Was the forging of ski tickets simply a teenage prank or could he have been involved in other illegal activities?

SEVEN

Two Concerns

But before getting into Ted's history in college, there were two major events that occurred during his teen years which I need to mention. Both are potentially significant relative to the development of a violent personality. Both happened within a year, maybe two, of each other.

On August 13, 1961, an eight-year-old girl named Ann Marie Burr disappeared from her home during the night. The family went to sleep at their usual bedtimes and when they woke up in the morning the girl was gone. Nobody had heard any noise that would suggest that somebody had come into the home, grabbed the girl from her bedroom, and carried her out of the house. She simply was there one moment and a few hours later she was gone and never seen again, alive or dead.

Ann Marie lived with her parents in a two-story home a couple of miles from Ted. Ted was 14 years old and he had a paper route at the time. He likely rode his bike past her house.

Her disappearance triggered a massive citywide search to find her or her body. Some believe that Ted may have kidnapped Ann Marie and then killed her. Others are not so sure. I was aware of the event and wanted to get Ted's impression of it. At first, I didn't believe that Ted had anything to do with it. I just wanted to get his take on it.

> *Ted, when you were a teenager, a little girl disappeared from her home. Someone appears to have talked her into coming out of her house during the night and when her family awoke in the morning she was gone. She was never seen again. What was your impression of it at that time?*
> Well, I didn't know anything about it.
> *But I heard there was a citywide search for her. She didn't live very far from where you lived and I'm sure it was the talk of the entire town. How could you not have known about it?*
> I was so involved in my school activities I didn't pay much attention to it.

It didn't make any sense that Ted wasn't aware of it since it was in the papers and was undoubtedly the talk around the dinner tables, at school, and in and out of the classrooms every day for weeks.

Ted dismissed any discussion about the girl's disappearance by claiming he didn't pay any attention to it. It's impossible that he didn't pay attention to the story. Dick Larsen, an associate editor of the Seattle Times, told me the entire town was up in arms about it. Dick said an event of that magnitude hadn't taken place in that town for years. Ted telling me he paid no attention to this raised a serious red flag in my mind regarding things he didn't seem to want to tell me. I began to consider that he might have had something to do with it, or at least he was more intimately interested in it than he would admit.

The other major event was that Ted first learned that he was illegitimate. He was about 13 or 14 years old at the time (date not certain, but it should be noted that if it was during this time, he would have been in middle school, and that might explain his withdrawal from social activities). Ted and his cousin John didn't get along very well during Ted's earlier years. Again, from things Ted said about his competitive relationship with John, it was clear that Ted was jealous of John.

One day Ted was having an argument with his cousin about who was going to have the best chance of success in the future. His cousin reportedly said he was going to go to a university in Europe and have an expensive car to drive around in. Ted said he was going to do the same. The argument heated up at which time his cousin reportedly told Ted that he wouldn't be able to do those things because he was illegitimate. This came as a complete shock to Ted and he began crying and yelling that it wasn't true. John took him to where family documents were kept and showed him his birth certificate. It said the father was unknown.

I was now fairly certain that his illegitimacy was a major issue and that this experience with his cousin added to any shyness and feelings of inferiority Ted might have already had up to this point in his life. Later, as part of this evaluation, when I called former girlfriends, I learned that Ted had brought up the issue of being illegitimate with them.

At this point of the evaluation I had a consistent theme that is often seen in people who become violent.

- He was illegitimate. He was seriously bothered by it but he wouldn't admit it to me.
- When his mother married John Bundy and had additional children, Ted likely felt left out, perhaps even rejected or abandoned. He never talked to me about family activities or vacations or of any fun things they did together.
- Ted's mother was religious and family activities revolved around the church. At one point, Ted played on the church basketball team and went to a church summer camp. Ted never said that when he was young, he had an interest in the church or in God. He said, "There was no puritanical governing in my home. The inhibitions were due to monetary factors, not religious ones." Ted never told me that he had a belief in God. In fact, he did not believe in a Christian God. If he was brought up in a religious home, at one time he would have been religious. What happened for him to lose that?
- He was lonely and shy as a child. In his teens, Ted had a sexual interest of looking down from his room into his neighbor's bathroom. This could lead to sexual curiosity and likely sexual fantasy. What did he do with the sexual urges that come alive during the teen years?
- The family was poor, his aunt was wealthy, and the cousin he was often around seemed headed for a good education and wealth, which Ted was unlikely to share in or have for himself.
- Ted avoided girls during his teen years, yet he dreamed of a future "beautiful co-ed." Was he starved for a relationship with a girl yet too shy to ask one out on a date? If so, how did he handle

the anger and frustration he would experience due to a fear of rejection? Or did he want a "beautiful co-ed" for the status it would confer on him, without consideration of the sexual or romantic relationship that would come with her entry into his life?
- His denial of being affected by learning he was illegitimate and of not having any interest regarding the disappearance of an eight-year-old girl who only lived a couple of miles from him were red flags.

A case for the development of a violent personality was beginning to show itself and a consistent picture was beginning to unfold. Clearly, evidence was found that Ted would likely have some psychological problems as an adult but, in fairness to Ted, I had not yet found the "smoking gun."

Ted was lonely as a child. His family was poor so he had to find ways to earn money if he wanted anything. He was shy and he lacked social skills. Something occurred when he was in junior high that caused him to stop pursuing activities with girls, which was likely to be, but was not necessarily, learning he was illegitimate. It could have just as easily have been the disappearance of Ann Marie Burr, if he had been involved in any way with it, as the two events happened in more or less the same time frame. Ted had two friends who supported him through his teenage years. He didn't date until he was a senior in high school. He reported no strong successes in life until he volunteered to do campaign work for his friends in high school who ran for school offices, and as a result was invited to be with them on skiing activities. The acquisition of friends through his work on the student body elections helped him begin to come out of his shell. Skiing with his friends was exceptionally good for him because it allowed him to be one of the guys. I later learned that it was also a traumatic experience because after a day on the slopes his friends went to dances while Ted went back home—alone.

EIGHT

College

Ted graduated from Wilson High School in the spring of 1965 with about a B average. He applied for and received a scholarship to the University of Puget Sound. Going to Puget Sound was born more out of necessity than as a first choice. Many of his friends went to the University of Washington or other universities or followed other pursuits. Ted had no car, minimal finances, and lived close to the college. It was really his only option.

In the fall of 1965, Ted began taking classes at the University of Puget Sound (UPS) but soon became dissatisfied. The problem for him there wasn't the lack of suitable classes or professors (he earned a B average), it was because he had no social life. He felt the students put too much emphasis on fraternity and sorority activities and he didn't have the money or the social standing to get into them. Ted said that, at the end of the school year, "I had to break away. I hadn't found what I wanted." It was clear that he didn't fit in and that bothered him. In the fall of 1966, following his freshman year at UPS, he transferred to the University of Washington.

There, as a sophomore at the University of Washington, Ted became interested in foreign affairs. He felt the U.S. government didn't deal justly with the People's Republic of China. His goal was to graduate from college, get a diplomatic position with the government, and work on improving trade with China. Ted wanted to have a position of authority that would allow him to work on promoting positive relationships between America and China. Importance, prestige, and wealth were his primary goals.

He was also concerned with the Watts riots (which took place in a section of Los Angeles in August 1965) and the way people were treating the Blacks. He said he enjoyed taking the counterpoint (playing devil's advocate) on issues when debating with people.

Ted said his year at the University of Puget Sound didn't give him what he was looking for and he had to "break away." But what was he looking for and what did he have to break away from? His lack of involvement with fraternities and sororities at UPS was likely due in part to not having a car and having very little money, and was compounded by his shyness.

Would his time at the University of Washington go better for him?

NINE

Marjorie and the University of Washington

The impression I had of Ted at this point of the interview was of a lonely boy seeking an identity. He hadn't found it in high school or at UPS and now he would try to find it at the University of Washington. His goals were impressive but his accomplishments minimal. He selected an Asian Studies program and he initially wanted to get in a fraternity.

> I was not a joiner of fraternities but I wanted social belonging. I didn't want to feel my identity was measured by a social group. I went through rush for four days but the social politics didn't do much for me, so I went into a dorm. There was too much emphasis on a social life and I wasn't interested in parties, clothes, or appearances. Plus, the cost of the fraternity was higher [than the dorms] and I didn't have the finances for it.
> *How did the dorm work out for you?*
> There were guys there who were in Asian Studies. I

got close to them. After that year I got a grant to go to Stanford for the summer.

What was your social life at the University of Washington?

At first, I was fully involved with my studies.

And then?

I went out with an Asian girl. It felt right because I was in Asian studies.

How did that relationship work out for you?

After we went out a couple of times her father had a talk with me. He was very nice about it. He said that he wanted his daughter to marry a boy who was Asian. He thought our backgrounds would conflict too much.

How did you feel about that?

It wasn't a problem. I understood where he was coming from. During spring quarter, I met a girl and we developed a very intense relationship. I had a Volkswagen at that time but at times we used her car because mine wasn't working very well.

What was her name?

Marjorie. [This is a pseudonym. Other authors have used the pseudonym Stephanie.]

Tell me about her.

We were both interested in intellectual topics and we got along very well. Her father was a vice president of an international company and they had a lot of money. She was an only child. Her parents were part of her everyday life. I got along with them.

How did that relationship work out?

She was well dressed. Well groomed. She had been a model at one time. She was very impressive and very appealing. I really enjoyed that. [Note: This answer was non-responsive. Or, perhaps, it was responsive, because Ted may have found the status she conferred on him to be more important than the actual functioning of the relationship.]

So, did it work out?

No. She got her feelings hurt easily and the relationship strained over petty matters. I had a busboy job at the Seattle Yacht Club. Marjorie was older than me and she expected more financial security than what I could provide. I had no savings and was often broke. I felt insecure about our relationship.

Did you and Marjorie get intimate? Did the two of you have sex?

She was the first girl I slept with but we didn't have intercourse. I don't think that either one of us was ready for it.

Didn't you go to a summer program?

I got a grant to go to Stanford University for their Asian Studies program. I went there during the summer of 1967.

How did you like it there?

It was really great. It was warm, the campus was beautiful, and the professors were very interesting.

Marjorie was from down in that area, wasn't she?

Yeah, but during that summer she was still up at the University of Washington. She was finishing up some classes that she needed to graduate.

How did it work out with Marjorie?

We began quarreling over things.

Did you finish your classes that summer at Stanford?

No. I couldn't focus on the lectures. I left without taking the final exams. After that summer, I felt I wasn't measuring up. Everything was just a bit too alien.

What did you do at that point?

I went back to the University of Washington to get into the fall semester.
That would be the fall semester of 1967, right?
Yes. I was going to take architecture but I couldn't get into the program so I went into Urban Studies.
And?
I dropped out. I got several incompletes. In January, I went skiing in Aspen and Vale but I got tired of it so I went to Philadelphia to see my grandparents. I also visited my uncle in Arkansas and then came back to Seattle and got a job as a busboy in a Hilton Hotel during the day and I was a night stocker in a Safeway store at night.

While Ted didn't specifically say so, it was clear that something significant, and possibly traumatic, happened between him and Marjorie when he was attending his summer classes at Stanford University. Asian studies and a career with the government was of paramount importance to him, but he dropped out of school both at Stanford and again when he tried going back to the University of Washington. Don Hull, who did the presentence report on Ted, told me of a lady who knew him during this period of time. I called her to get her impressions of Ted. It was what she told me that convinced me there was a lot more to Ted than what he was telling me.

TEN

A Conversation with Sybil Ferris

Mrs. Ferris was an elderly nurse who knew Ted quite well. I identified myself and explained the reason for my phone call. I said I was doing an evaluation for the court on Ted Bundy and that I would appreciate any information she could give me regarding what he was like when she knew him. She was very open about Ted.

> I'm a woman of 70 years and I know what goes on but he doesn't have it.

What a powerful statement! Here is a woman who immediately gets to the point. The tone of her voice suggested she had a very unfavorable impression of Ted.

What was he like when you first met him?

> I don't know if he was high on dope or liquor, but he was sure a peculiar person.
>
> *In what way?*
>
> He was going with a girl from San Francisco. He would portray himself to be a really big politician to try to get in good with her family. He borrowed Havilland China and Sterling Silver and linen from me, and he had her there for dinner, and he was going to show her what a fine cook he was, and what a man he would be around the house. He got her drunk and they spent the night there.

This information is very powerful. Ted had said that he wasn't interested in parties, clothes, or appearances. Either Ted was lying or Mrs. Ferris was wrong. I assumed it was Ted because I frequently caught him denying things that others said were true.

> He borrowed my car several times to go out on night trips. I was scared to death when he was gone. There was something up because he just wasn't running true to form of where he was going or what he was doing. He got him a job at the Olympic Hotel and went through the men's employee lockers and found some old tuxedos. It was waiter's clothes: pants, coat, and other things. He got them fixed up and he would dress himself up as if he were a headwaiter in some restaurant. He lived for a short while with an elderly couple and they were going to go to Norway. They finally had to ask him to move.

Again, a contradiction of what Ted said about clothes not being important. Theft and the need to impress people painted a completely different picture of Ted than he had previously indicated.

> He got a job at Safeway for a short while and just quit, not even going back to work to tell them he was leaving.

This suggests impulsivity and difficulty with commitments. Ted was a thief and he was irresponsible. The important point here is that these things were occurring while he and Marjorie still had a good relationship. This change in Ted's behavior from how he described himself in high school could likely not have taken place in such a short period of time after he left high school. And it would not have been due to breaking up with Marjorie. This statement by Mrs. Ferris suggests a critical flaw in Ted's personality. Continuing, she said,

> He borrowed a hundred dollars from me. I tried to get him to pay me back but he always had some reason why he couldn't pay me back right then. He never did pay me back.

Again, problems with honesty and responsibility.

> One of the men Ted was going around with got some furniture from me to sell for me but I never got the money for it. He is a very, very peculiar boy. He was just kind of sneaking around. He'd be on the telephone when you'd least expect him to be on the telephone. He would tell me he was going to be one place and he would be somewhere else.

It was not just one or two behaviors and untruths that made her uncomfortable with Ted. While this is only one person's opinion, it is a very negative one. This suggested that there was something very wrong with Ted which undoubtedly extended back through his teenage years and possibly into his childhood. Her use of the word "sneaky" and the phrases "I was scared to death when he was gone" and "he was sure a peculiar person" is indicative of a person who has a personality disorder. This suggests that Ted had some sort of a secret life that he kept hidden from her—and also from me and others who attempted to evaluate him. There was clearly a secret side to Ted. Did secret mean "dark"? Did Ted have a dark side to him during those early years with Marjorie? If so, was she aware of it? If he had a private life, what purpose did it serve him? I could see why he wouldn't tell me things during the evaluation. He didn't want me to be aware of any behavioral or personality problems to which I could refer to conclude he was violent. Mrs. Ferris continued,

> He left the area on a plane one time. He said he was going to Colorado to be a ski instructor there. Something happened and he came back.
> He went to Pennsylvania and drove his uncle's

The 1976 Psychological Assessment of Ted Bundy • 65

> Cadillac and came back flat broke looking for a job.
> All in all, he's just a very weird boy.
> I talked to his mother once. I asked her if she would appeal to him as a man to return the hundred dollars I loaned him. His mother said, "He doesn't live here anymore and we're not responsible for anything he does."

What does that mean? Does it simply mean that her mother was saying she wasn't responsible for Ted's behavior because he was not living at home, or did it go beyond that?

> He would use a British accent.

Ted had told me that when he listened to the weekly adventure serials on the radio, he would pretend he was the hero in the story. The same was true when he listened to political speeches on the radio and memorized some of the things he heard. This sounds like he was pretending to be somebody important to impress, but who? Marjorie? Her parents? Someone else I had yet to identify? Or just everyone?

> I worked with him at the Seattle Yacht Club when he was a busboy and I got him a job at the Olympus Hotel. Then he got a job at Safeway. Then he got into politics. I called and told them he was a strange boy and a little on the crooked side.

This statement emphasizes her distrust of him. It isn't often that a person will call a perspective employer to complain about a job seeker.

> He was six weeks at the Yacht Club and they let him go. He wasn't supposed to eat the food, but he was always in the pantry eating all the fresh foods and whipped cream he could get and all the fancy foods he could eat. He would grab them and take them to his locker. He was always in trouble with them.

Here again are examples of his poverty, his dishonesty, his propensity to steal, and his sneaky nature.

> *Did he ever seem to be an easy person to get close to, or was he distant?*
> Oh, he was distant! He had kind of a running game of his own. He didn't have too much to do with his family. He borrowed my car a couple of times saying he was going home. Ted never talked about his family or showed much affection for them. I moved him twice using my car to haul his things to a new location. Ted spent quite a bit of time at a friend's house, an antique dealer who had been in prison. Ted told me he was studying Chinese at the University of Washington. When the draft seemed to get close, he told me he was going to skip out and go to Taiwan.

The picture she was painting didn't sound like a college student who wants to work for the government to help improve relationships between America and China. As Mrs. Ferris continued her account of Ted, she was describing psychopathic personality traits.

> I have been suspicious from the day those two girls were killed at Lake Sammamish with that "Ted." I remember seeing him in an Albertson's store in Green Lake with a cast on his arm. I was going to do something about it, but living alone I was afraid to do more than what I had already done.
> *Did he seem strange? Mentally ill or a criminal?*
> He seemed to have mental problems, although I couldn't place him in any diagnostic category. He had ways of getting money. He had a very expensive overcoat with a fur collar that came from the Yankee Peddler, one of the men's best dress shops in the University District. He had a key to the men's dormitory at the University of Washington long after he left there. He carried the key with him and he used to go in there and sleep on the lounge couches when he didn't have any place to go and he would take clothing and things from the dorm.

She was drawing a picture of an irresponsible person who seemed consistently involved with illegal and secretive activities. A very important point in what she was saying was that she was afraid of him. A person with psychopathic traits who incites fear often has violent traits. This was part of the smoking gun I was searching for. She concluded,

> I was willing to give him the benefit of the doubt because I felt he needed help. I felt there was something very, very wrong in his life. It seemed as if he was quite an unloved child the way that it hit me. I just kind of felt I could help him, but I finally decided I was just knocking my head against a wall and I just had to stop it and I couldn't have him taking my car and keeping it out until 3:00 a.m. or 4:00 a.m. in the morning and telling me he would be back at midnight and me sitting up waiting.
> *Where did he say he was taking the car?*
> He told me he was going on trips. He would be gone all these hours and would come back all hepped up. He did this two or three times. I thought he might be trafficking dope.

This fascinating conversation with Mrs. Ferris was very revealing. She, being a trained nurse, was experienced with medical and psychological problems. What I was learning from her was more consistent with a violent personality than of a typical college student working toward a law degree.

I next wanted to talk to Marjorie.

ELEVEN

A Conversation with Marjorie

Ted said his goal for the future was to graduate from college and find a beautiful co-ed. When Marjorie came into his life, she was everything he had dreamed of. He fell deeply in love with her. She was at a higher station in life than him. She was older, more experienced with life, and came from a successful family. If he was this shy boy who didn't date in high school, what did she see in him that made it worth her time to go out with him? And, if at first there was something to the relationship, what made it change?

I called her and explained that I was doing a psychological assessment for the court and asked if she would be willing to talk about her relationship with Ted. She was quite open.

What did you like about him?
I was caught up by his ability to talk. You know, he could just off the cuff come out with anything and it would sound good. And he wrote fantastic letters.

. . .

This was likely Ted's greatest asset. His excellent verbal skills attracted people. I had noticed this as well. It is often assumed that if a person can speak intelligently then there must be an inner strength to back it up. She continued,

> He put a great deal of importance on a person's ability and intelligence, in their quickness of mind.
> *Did he ever seem to be involved with anything illegal?*
> I didn't know of anything. If I had, I'd probably have been real scared. I'm a real chicken.
> *Did he seem to have any friends?*
> No, and that was weird too. There were none that I knew of.

This is interesting. Ted had a couple of friends in high school and he said that when he was living in the dorm during his sophomore year prior to going to Stanford University he got close to students who were in the Asian Studies program. He had left the University of Puget Sound because he couldn't find friends. He thought that the University of Washington would cure that. Evidently it didn't.

> *What did he do in his spare time?*
> I don't know. He had a bike and he rode around on his bike. He also went skiing every once in a while.
> *Was he good?*
> Oh yes, he was very athletic.

What was Ted like as you saw him at the time you were going with him?
He was athletic and he was brilliant but he was not terribly social. He always had sort of a bowing manner, always trying to get people to believe that he was humble and that he wouldn't walk on anybody's toes. Like he was pleased to be in somebody's presence. He seemed to have a great deal of insecurity and lack of finesse in dealing with other people.
Insecure in what way?
He was a very passive person. He had an oddity which I thought sort of went with this lack of confidence. It was a put on. His actions were to make people feel, "poor Ted, sweet little Ted." Yet I think he had this feeling that he was very… sort of debonair.
Like he…
Understood the world.
Did it ever seem like he was hurt by a girl?
Not that I knew of. I felt he hadn't had much contact with women until he got involved with me. We pretty much experienced each other together that way.

This was an interesting portrayal of Ted. He felt he understood the world yet he lacked confidence. He was very intelligent, a good skier, and a good writer, yet his passivity and not believing in himself seemed to result in him putting on a pretense to get people to like him.

In the beginning, did he ever sleep with you and not have sex?
Did Ted tell you that?
Yeah, he did.
We did a lot of that. I wasn't experienced at all with sex and I wasn't on any birth control methods and I didn't know if I wanted to do it. We did a lot of playing around but it didn't culminate in sex.
Did it ever seem that Ted just wanted sex or do you feel that he was in love with you?
He never made me feel like it was just a physical thing. I believed he was in love with me. I was very turned on but I wasn't experienced. I didn't know what I wanted to do.
Did he ever seem to get frustrated with that?
I guess he did. Yeah, I'm sure he did.

Marjorie was Ted's first serious romantic relationship. Marjorie portrayed Ted as a loner who was very insecure. It appeared that Ted was deeply in love with Marjorie and he was centering his life on her and on a career in Asian Studies. That could be a dangerous combination if things didn't work out in the relationship.

It appeared that Ted was still exceptionally shy in college, yet he was able to impress people by his intelligence. It was as if he had the capacity for success but not the personality to go with it. It's as if he was acting out a part to convince people that he was more than he himself believed he was. If he put a great deal of effort into showing a fake personality to others, what then was going on that he was not showing? Was he putting all of his marbles in one basket with his life in politics and his "beautiful co-ed"? If so, what would happen if the bottom fell out?

> *It's been said that Ted was an angry person. Did you see any of that in him?*
> No, Ted didn't show a lot of anger when I first got to know him. We were truly in love with each other at that time. It was a great emotional relationship.

The impression I get from this is that Ted was sincerely trying to develop a relationship with Marjorie. But what about the conversation with Mrs. Ferris? Did Ted have some sort of a secret life that he completely hid from Marjorie but was only partly able to hide from Mrs. Ferris?

> *Can you say anything about his relationship with his mother?*
> I was under the impression that he cared about his mother and he felt sorry for her. He felt she was a competent person who got messed up with a nothing of a father. I think that he liked his mother a little bit because he felt that she was sweet.
> He seemed to adore his little brother, his younger brother. That seemed to be the only reason, when we were together, why he went home. It was because his brother was smart.
> *Ted said that you and he would have some arguments or quarrels. What was he like in those situations?*
> Oh, pitifully weak! This was my main criticism of him after the year and a half of our relationship. He

kowtowed to me. He wasn't strong. He wasn't real masculine. If I got mad at him because he did something, he sort of felt apologetic about it.

He wouldn't stand up for himself. There was no use getting mad because the person didn't react. And the things I got mad for were primarily that he lied. It wasn't that he out and out lied. He fibbed. It wasn't necessary that he had to be like that. It wasn't actually that he had done a bad thing in his mind. It was that he was saying something he knew would sound good to me.

For example?
Instead of saying his pants came from Sears, he said he bought them at a high-class store. He would make something to appear to be what it wasn't to impress me. Of course, we came from very different backgrounds. He was very concerned about those things, and about his lack of experience. I had experience in small things like restaurants and the things that would be important to a young coed.

In the beginning of our relationship he was always reverting back to the need to sort of beg because he didn't have anything. He didn't have a car. He, in fact, would sometimes tell me he hadn't eaten that day because he didn't have enough money. It never seemed to bother him that he was using people.

Would he borrow from you?
He never did off me because I never gave him a cent. Sometimes I felt he was spending his last dime to buy me something.

Given what she was telling me, Ted was a phony. This reinforced what Mrs. Ferris had told me. Ted was acting like he had remarkable goals for his future—which he actually may have had—but he had no way to deliver. He clearly planned on Marjorie being there with him when he finally succeeded and got the life he always talked about, the life that he and his cousin John had argued over. However, what I was learning was that Ted's personality was shallow and superficial. It appeared that he was a good actor, but only for short periods of time. He could repeat a personality script as if he was in a play on stage, but it was only a character part he had taught himself, and he didn't have the depth of an actual personality behind it. Using his intelligence, he had conformed his image to what he felt would impress others. Is this why many people believed that Ted could not possibly have killed anyone? Cleary, he had not succeeded in impressing everyone because Marjorie and Mrs. Ferris could see through the façade.

How did your relationship with Ted end?
I began cutting it off in letters at first, before it ended. He knew it was coming.
How did he respond to this?
Oh, sort of begging. I told him it was never going to work, that he wasn't the kind of person I needed. I loved him dearly but I couldn't exist with him. I just wasn't comfortable with the things he did and the way he kowtowed to me. I just didn't feel he was straight with me all the time. I pushed him away and I cut off my ties with him. This was about 1966 or 1967. It was in my junior or senior year in college.
What was his reaction?
He cried. He *cried.* He was really falling apart in

front of me. That's when he went out to Philadelphia to run away from the whole thing. It was to go to school. And I would call him when I needed attention.

When you finally cut if off, what did he do?
I don't know. He left. I took him to the airport or something. He called me a couple of times. He sent me flowers and some cards.

After you and Ted broke up, the two of you continued to talk on the phone from time to time. What was your impression of his life?
He floundered around for years and years and years, never completing anything, going from one place to another, getting involved in all the wrong things.

Such as?
The politicking. He was a member of a group in the Republican party that would go around to the opponent when they made speeches. He would tape them and rephrase the speech and use it against the opponent. There was a Black man running for something in the state, I believe. Ted helped him by driving for miles in his VW, and I just didn't trust any of that stuff.

I'm pretty conservative. I got the feeling that he was sometimes associating with people who used drugs. He told me he did that but he said he didn't try them himself. This, of course, was in the early stage of our relationship.

When he was going to University of Washington and Stanford?
Yes.

. . .

Ted had told me he dropped out of college at Stanford University because he couldn't focus on the lectures. He had said, "I left without taking the final exams. After that summer I felt I wasn't measuring up. Everything was just a bit too alien." Clearly, he had avoided telling me that this was because of Marjorie cutting off the relationship. When I interviewed others, I became convinced that Ted was never able to recover from their breakup.

However, they weren't completely finished with each other. They continued to call each other from time to time, just to talk. Marjorie would call Ted when she felt lonely or was simply curious about how his life was going. Ted kept in touch with Marjorie but he never told me why. Was this only to continue a friendship or was there more to it? I would soon learn that there was an underlying motive and strategy that Ted was working on.

TWELVE

Ted's First Trip to Philadelphia

Ted left Stanford and gave up his Chinese Studies. He never went back to them again. He returned to the University of Washington for the fall quarter of 1967 but he couldn't settle down and got several incompletes. In January of 1968 he left the area.

> I had to regroup. I had saved money from my busboy job. I went skiing at Aspen until I became tired of it. Then I called my aunt in Philadelphia and went there. Then I visited my uncle Jack in Arkansas for a week or so and I came back to Seattle.
> I was a busboy at the Hilton Hotel and a stocker at Safeway at night. I met a friend who worked in the Art Fletcher campaign. I got involved with it and I became chairman of a youth group in Seattle. I later worked for the New Majority for the Rockefeller campaign. I was still working at night in Safeway.
> I saw Marjorie a couple of times. I had to sneak into

the taverns because I wasn't yet 21 years old. I was in the process of rebuilding and she was about to graduate and go into a stockbroker's firm. So, we were worlds apart.

At times the information Ted gave me seemed rehearsed. He stammered and took longer to respond when asked questions he didn't seem prepared for.

> I really enjoyed politics but after the nomination of Nixon I went back to the Fletcher campaign. I became his personal driver for him and his wife. I was somewhat of a counselor to him and I would critique his speeches and his political policies.

The Fletcher campaign was short-lived because Fletcher lost. Did Ted really reach such a level of trust with the candidate that he was allowed to read his speeches and critique his political policies? Not likely.

Up to this time in his life, Ted had not had sex with a woman other than the times he and Marjorie would "play around in bed." Ted enjoyed his work in the Fletcher campaign but it didn't go well.

> The campaign was a disaster. My social life and political life intertwined.
> One time we were out of town during the campaign.

I went to a party as a representative of Fletcher and I was picked up by a woman and taken to her house. I was very drunk. During the night the girl came down and hopped in bed with me. That was my first sexual encounter. This girl was separated from her husband. She was hysterical.
I had slept with Marjorie half a dozen times with no clothes on and we petted heavily but we didn't have sex since she wasn't on the pill.
Did it bother you not to have intercourse with Marjorie?
No. She smoked and I didn't. I liked classical music and she was more into rock.

I'm not sure what Marjorie's smoking and the fact they liked different music had to do with whether or not he was bothered by the incomplete sexual experiences with her. This was one of the times when he seemed caught off guard with the question and didn't think it through before giving an answer.

Did you ever borrow money from her or use her credit cards?
No, I didn't.
What did you do next?
In September of 1968 I went back to Seattle and I went to work in a shoe store. I wanted to go back to school. I wanted to go into law but I wasn't ready to go back to the University of Washington.
What stopped you?
It was just the memories of the failures I had there.
What did you decide to do?

I went back east again. I went to Temple University in Philadelphia and I majored in political science. I had understood that I could get a degree in law without having to have a bachelor's degree.
I take it you didn't stay there.
There was too much crime and violence. The new buildings had no windows. The playgrounds had barbed wire around them.
What classes did you take?
I took classes on the nature of student populations to find something to get the community involved. I gained an appreciation of law-abiding Blacks.
Why did you choose to go to Temple University?
I lived in Philadelphia when I was young and I had some relatives there.

Why did you leave the university? Why not continue going to school there?
I went one semester and I got B's in my classes. When I learned that I couldn't get a law degree without getting my bachelor's degree first I lost interest so I left.
What did you do?
I took a transport car across the country to San Francisco. I'd been writing poems to Marjorie. I contacted her when I got there. I was there about five days and we spent a lot of time together. We went on a trip up the coast together.
How did it work out?
There wasn't a deep romantic love between us.

This must have been very frustrating for Ted. He couldn't end the relationship with Marjorie even though he was never satisfied with her. And Marjorie couldn't seem to permanently end it either. His statement about there not being a deep romantic love between them suggested that he was still in love with her but she was not in love with him.

THIRTEEN

Liz Kendall and the Fall of 1969

Ted returned to Seattle and got an apartment which he lived in for the next six years.

I met Liz Kendall that fall [1969]. I have a lot of pleasant memories of her and her three-year-old daughter. I had my own apartment but I stayed in her apartment for weeks at a time. We took a trip that Christmas to see her parents in Utah. Her father was a doctor. She and I had an intense relationship. In June of 1970 I returned to the University of Washington and majored in psychology. I got my BS degree in psychology in June of 1972. I got a part time job in a warehouse delivering medical equipment. It was a very tranquil period for me. It was a growing period as well.
How did the relationship work out?
She wanted to get married, and there were times that I did as well. But when it came right down to it, I

wasn't quite in the mood. We got a marriage license but I hadn't graduated from college and I wasn't a wage earner so I didn't follow through. I deeply loved her. My being able to go back to college was largely due to her support. She frequently supported me, in fact.

What kept you from marrying her? You had some finances coming in, you spent a lot of time at her apartment, and she was supporting you in college. What was wrong with the relationship that kept you from marrying her?

Liz didn't fit the mold of a politician's wife and she had a daughter. She stopped taking her birth control pills at the recommendation of her doctor. It was just to give her body a rest. She got pregnant early in 1972 and she decided to have an abortion. I didn't urge her to or try to stop her. She had the abortion. We both had deep, deep regrets about not having a child.

During the first two and a half years I ate almost all my meals at her house. She gave me $100 for school at one time.

Did the relationship continue to go well? This would be the spring of 1972. Right?

Yes. I had an emotional falling out. I can't think of any event that precipitated it. There was no arguing or yelling. It was that Liz needed constant reinforcement. She needed love over and over again.

What were some of the things that caused a conflict between you?

One of them was her ideas of how to raise a child. She had no firm idea of how to do it. My position was that a time out was the best solution when a girl showed disrespect toward her mother. Liz exploded on her daughter. She would grab her daughter and shake her.

I was the object of their anger. I became insensitive to Liz. I began forgetting her birthday and not showing up for dinner when she expected me to be there. But we always came back together.

Were there other things she did that made you angry?
I think I may have blanked out things that I was angry about. However, there were no major things—none that lasted more than one day.

However, there was one occasion when she had somebody over to her apartment. She was drunk and they had sex. I felt terribly hurt. I went home and sulked. My world was destroyed! THAT WAS THE LAST STRAW!

His statement was slow and firm. At this point, Ted went silent and stared into space. He was reliving the event. There was a dramatic change in his body language. His voice was stronger, he was very angry and, while his face was turned toward me, he looked beyond me. What I saw was a very hurt man. He had just finished telling me there was nothing major that made him angry with Liz. Now he reported an *extremely* emotional event. It appeared that this memory was one that he couldn't suppress and, once it came into his mind, couldn't avoid talking about. After several seconds he regained his composure. He looked at me and said,

But we got back together and we both cried. That was the only time she was unfaithful.

As it turned out, it wasn't the only time she showed an interest in another man. And it wasn't the only time Ted would show intense anger during my interviews with him.

FOURTEEN

Graduation from College and Seattle Harborview Hospital

At this point of the evaluation it appeared there were two sides to the personality of Ted Bundy. He was intelligent and could be impressive. He talked of wanting to help the poor. He was able to get people to like him, some so much they complained to the Salt Lake Sheriff's Office that they had likely arrested the wrong person.

However, he wasn't sticking with anything. He had given up on Chinese studies. He promised marriage to his girlfriend Liz with seemingly no intention of following through with it. Mrs. Ferris reported strong suspicions that there was something wrong with him and that Ted needed help. Among other things she said he was a thief.

Ted clearly worked hard to mask his undesirable side from others. He was a private person and Liz, who loved Ted, didn't see the dark side of him. Liz didn't understand him. Marjorie felt that Ted hid himself from her and, even after a couple of years of their relationship, felt she still didn't know him.

Ted had some admirable traits but was still not having consistent success in relationships, in employment, or in life.

Even so, now that he had graduated from college, perhaps some opportunities would open up for him. And maybe he would keep his promises to Liz.

In June of 1972, Ted graduated from the University of Washington, obtaining a Bachelor's of Science degree in psychology. Liz gave him a yellow six-man rubber raft that the two of them could enjoy when they went on picnics to the Yakima River. (This raft would later play a major role in demonstrating the violent side of Ted.)

Ted said,

> I got a summer job at the Seattle Crisis Clinic doing counseling. I got a lot of personal growth and maturity from it. I began to feel cocky and I started showing up at Liz's apartment less often.

What does Ted mean by cocky? Does it mean that now that he had completed college, he didn't need Liz any longer? Or was there something else that made him feel "cocky" and independent?

> I got involved with a couple of girls at the center. I slept with both of them. I was deceitful with Liz. I did the typical bad guy thing.

What did he mean by "the typical bad guy thing"? How typical was this behavior he spoke of?

What did he say to these girls to entice them to sleep

with him? Ted was now playing around with four girls: Liz and Marjorie and the two girls he worked with at the clinic. This appears to be somewhat psychopathic.

> One of the girls was named Kimberly. Liz discovered that I was seeing Kim. One night I took Kim to a restaurant and when I got back to my apartment Liz was there. She was hysterical. I saw her like that a couple of times. Both of the times I had gone out with another girl.
> Liz saw Kim's car and she went into a state of physical shock. I was deeply ashamed that I had hurt her. I told Kim about it. I went to Liz's apartment. Her daughter was there. Liz sat there staring. She was like a zombie. I got her best friend to come and watch after her. I felt extremely bad about it so I told Kim it just wasn't working out and I broke it off with her.

My next phone call was to Kim.

FIFTEEN

Kimberly

Kimberly, referred to as Kim by her friends, was an attractive 23-year old who had graduated college and was doing an internship in counseling at the Harborview Mental Health Center in Seattle in the summer of 1972. Ted had graduated from the University of Washington with a Bachelor's degree in psychology and was looking for work. Both Ted and Kim were offered intern positions at the clinic where they, along with other interns, would work with the mentally ill. Ted told me he didn't like it there because he had to work with schizophrenics, but Kim said they worked with patients with anxiety and depression as well as schizophrenia.

Prior to this internship, Ted had worked for several months on a crisis line with Ann Rule, a writer of crime stories. At the time of my evaluation of Ted, she was a strong supporter of his. At Ted's request, she sent me a copy of a poem he wrote to her while he was in jail. She had gotten to know him fairly well over the months they worked together, so much so that when Ted was arrested in Salt Lake, she was convinced by what she had seen when working with him that there was no way that he could be guilty.

Kim was in training meetings and therapy sessions with Ted and other interns, and she and the others had the opportunity to watch each other in practice.

When I called Kim, she said she was initially impressed with Ted's good looks and his ability to talk, and he seemed confident and self-assured. She admired his mind. He had the ability to analyze things, to think things through.

Ted seemed to like Kim because she was attractive, fairly wealthy, and came from an influential family.

Ted hadn't been at the center for very long before people changed their opinions of him. Kim said they were critical of him because he didn't follow the normal intern schedule and "he came and went as he chose." Kim said,

> In therapy, he was harsh and cold and people were dismayed. He showed anger toward women and others. He lacked understanding of the clients.

She said he showed self-confidence outwardly, but he had strong feelings of inferiority underneath.

Kim started dating Ted but said, "The relationship was strained. It was as if there was a power struggle between us." They would plan an event and Kim assumed that Ted would take charge and set up the arrangements. However, when it came time for the date to take place, she would find that Ted hadn't done what he said he would do. She said, "As we got closer to it, I would suddenly find the burden was on my shoulders."

I asked her if she would feel comfortable about discussing

any sexual activities between them. It was a very personal question and one I generally don't ask people to talk about. However, I thought it was important in this case because of Ted's crime. Kim said,

> A couple of times when he made sexual advances, it was a real mental and physical struggle about who was going to get their way. It wasn't that I would tell him I didn't want sex. It was the timing. It was a putdown to him, an absolute putdown. I really had to do a lot of fast talking because it wasn't appropriate at that particular time, in that place. That seemed to be more and more of a challenge to him, as if he was trying to break down the barriers. To win was sort of a conquest of his.

Kim described a time when Ted took her on a picnic to a local river. They traveled down the highway until they reached a point where Ted turned off the main road onto a dirt road and then turned off onto another less frequented dirt road. Kim was impressed that Ted knew this out of the way place for such an event. It seemed obvious that Ted wasn't looking for a new place to have the picnic. He had been there previously. There were no houses or other indicators that many people went there. He soon turned off on yet another dirt road. Ted stopped by a large tree that was close to the river. The branches extended out over the river and they were large enough that a person could climb out and jump in.

It was a hot day. They lay in the shade of the tree and talked and drank some wine.

> He said he wanted me to climb up into the tree and jump in. This is where the antagonism started. It was a stupid thing to do in the first place and then to try to force me to do it….

She told Ted she didn't want to do it. He kept after her and finally she jumped from the bank into the river.

> I got in the water thinking that if I was already in the water, he wouldn't keep pressing me to climb up in the tree and jump in. He got in the water with me and dunked my head under. He tried to untie the top of my bathing suit. It was a pretty swift current and I didn't want to lose the top of my bathing suit.

Kim said Ted held her head under the water for a long time. When he allowed her to come up, she confronted him: "What are you trying to do? Drown me?"

> He laughed and dunked me under again. I didn't think of it as if I was going to drown. I didn't think he was trying to kill me. I thought, he doesn't realize what he's doing.

He pushed her head under water three times and he kept trying to undo her bathing suit. To stop him from doing that she tied her top in so many knots she had to cut it off when she got home.

Her statement that Ted didn't seem to realize what he was doing seemed extremely important. Some of the violent inmates I worked with in prison told me of times when they would go into a fantasy while attacking their victim. They said the depth of the fantasy was such that they were unaware of what was going on around them.

There was another girl I talked to who was a friend of Liz's and was acquainted with Ted at Harborview. She said that Ted seemed to "space out" when he was stressed. It appeared from her comment that Ted dissociated. If so, where did he go in his mind?

When Ted and Kim got out of the river, they had sex. It evidently was on the ground and not on a blanket because Kim remembered small cuts and scratches on her back and neck from being on the ground. She said the sex was consensual but it was as if Ted was raping her. It was,

> … very intense, very aggressive. It was as though I really didn't think he was conscious of what he was doing because it wasn't a bonding situation. I was just a body lying there is all. It wasn't as if we were doing something together. Something was being done to me. It was sheer terror. It flashed in my mind that nobody else was around here.

SIXTEEN

Confirmation of Ted's Violent Personality

Psychologically healthy people have open and relatively close relationships with others. Killers, on the other hand, tend to be secretive, distant, and angry. A healthy person interacts with people in a positive manner. A killer fantasizes about relationships he wants but is unable to obtain. A healthy person is true to his feelings. A killer hides his violent emotions and puts on an act of normalcy.

A constant struggle takes place in the killer's mind between his violent thoughts and emotions and his fear of who he is becoming. He acts the part of normalcy as if he is playing out a role on stage in front of a large audience. He shows people what he thinks they want to see.

However, his deeper violent emotions are always just under the surface and are easily brought out into the open. He attempts to hide his dark side but as it grows stronger, he has to be even more careful in what he allows others to see. He becomes fearful that a thought, a word, or an action might slip out and give him away.

Up to this point in my evaluation I had three people now who said they at first had a very positive impression of Ted

Bundy but it didn't take long before they began to see a dark side to him. It was clear that Ted was not the "normal" college student he wanted others to see him as. He had been aggressive and he appeared to dissociate. It was clear that Ted wasn't in control of his emotions during the summer of 1972. But still, I didn't have a "smoking gun" that would convince me that Ted was not just different, he was violent.

Kim was initially impressed with Ted but she had a roommate who thought that Ted was weird. She had a girlfriend who thought that Ted was pretentious and a phony.

One of the primary issues between Kim and Ted was his feelings of inferiority. Marjorie had seen it years before and it was one of the reasons she had ended the relationship. Now that Ted had graduated from college with a degree in psychology, he had the opportunity for a career in mental health, and he still had Liz who believed in him. It would suggest that he had proven himself to some degree. However, Kim related,

> He told somebody at work that I was of the status class or something like that and that he felt inferior to me. He apologized all over the place for his background. I could not convince him that his background was not that relevant. He felt inferior and I think maybe that's why the intellectual battle occurred. It seemed as though he was striving for some means of proving himself.

Kim felt that Ted put her up on a pedestal and then would try to knock her off. She described his behavior as different from other guys she dated.

> He always wore dark clothes, even in the summer. He wore turtleneck sweaters. He was a night person. He would show up without telling me he was coming, sometimes at midnight.

There was one thing she said that began to convince me that there were some very unusual aspects about Ted Bundy. I asked Kim if there was anything that seemed puzzling about Ted when she was going with him. She said,

> Well, at times he would take me for a drive in the hills by Lake Sammamish and he would drive around and around. I would ask him about it and he would say he was looking for an aunt. It didn't make any sense because there were only cabins there. It certainly was not residential by any means. It was in the woods.

They were in Kim's car and Ted was driving. The dirt roads they were on were bad. Kim became frightened because, "I kept telling him to slow down but he wouldn't." Finally, she insisted that he slow down. The reaction she got from him frightened her.

> He really reacted and he started yelling at me. I couldn't figure out where that kind of a reaction was coming from. His temper was way out of line. To tell me to shut up was one thing but he really exploded at me. That was the first display of temper I had seen. It was inappropriate. It wasn't as though I was sitting there nagging at him. It was just one comment. After that I didn't know what to say.

For the most part Ted kept his relationships with other women a secret but Liz eventually found out about Kim. One evening when Kim and Ted were at a restaurant, Liz discovered it. Ted left the restaurant to go back to his apartment to get something. Liz was there and she was hysterical. Kim said, "He told me Liz was hysterical and was going to kill herself. He said she was jealous and was going to commit suicide." At that point, he ended the relationship with Kim.

Before bringing the conversation with Kim to an end, I had one more important question. One woman told me about how Ted would seem to space out when he was stressed. Would he also dissociate during sex? If so, it would suggest that fantasy sex was extremely important to him. Either he couldn't enjoy sex without it or he may have been reliving a very powerful sexual experience during sexual activity. If so, sex with a current partner was a method he used to allow him to more fully relive the earlier event. This is a serious problem if the current sexual activity touches on violence. I asked Kim if there were times when Ted seemed to dissociate during sex. She said,

Ah, yeah, there were. One time when we were making love Ted seemed out of it. He was spaced out. He seemed to be in some kind of a sexual fantasy. He had his arm over my throat and it was choking me and I couldn't breathe. I couldn't bring him out of it. Finally, he stopped.

Her statement that she couldn't bring him out of the sexual fantasy suggests dissociation during sexual activity. When Ted was investigated by the police, they found the book *The Joy of Sex* in his apartment. There was a section in it that said the most exciting sexual activity could be achieved through bondage of the victim.

I now had about all I needed to convince me that Ted had a violent streak to his personality. The psychological test results had revealed that Ted was intelligent and didn't have a psychotic disorder, but that he wasn't going to reveal his deeper emotions. The people I talked to independently gave their impressions of him without colluding with others but they all said basically the same thing. Ted had a dark side to him.

However, my psychological investigation wasn't finished. Ted spoke of getting back together with Marjorie during the summer of 1973.

SEVENTEEN

Fall of 1972

Ted did not enjoy working at the mental health center and he left in September of 1972 to work for the Governor Evans' re-election campaign as a volunteer, saying he admired the man and felt close to his issues. Governor Evans was re-elected. Ted was in his element once again and he made a good impression on the officiators of the campaign.

At the beginning of 1973, the governor had a victory celebration. Ted took Liz but she went off on her own and drank because she wasn't comfortable around large groups of people. This was a concern for Ted because people asked where she was. On the other hand, Ted may have felt more comfortable with her not beside him because he didn't see her as a politician's wife.

He also said he could have had a job in Olympia, Washington, but didn't want to leave Liz. He said he was able to obtain a contract for a three-month study on misdemeanants but he couldn't remember the specific purpose of the study. He didn't finish it and left by giving a verbal report of his findings but not the expected written report. He said he started out with an optimistic attitude but became discouraged over the lack of funds and time to do the project.

Ted said he worked for a month for the assistant to the Director of Crime Commission. He felt the group he was working with had been pulled together by the mayor to have a crime commission because Chicago had one. He looked for significant issues to study and decided that white collar crime was probably a good one. He started looking at rape and rape prevention. However, he said he didn't stay there for long either because the pay was not good and the commission was an advisory board with no executive power.

He got a good paying job to study recidivism, which was a three-month contract. He felt he could have settled down with government work because he had "friends in influential positions." However, he got a more attractive offer towards the end of the contract and I believe he didn't complete this contract as well.

He then started working for the State Republican party and stated he was active in trying to make changes. He went to a lot of parties and post-election activities. He had thoughts of reconstructing the party—he had a lot of ideas regarding campaign services including polling, which he said he had learned from his psychology class. He wrote papers on it and the chairman was impressed. He got a better paying job on an open contract. He got along well with Ross Davis, Chairman of the Washington State Republican Party, and became his assistant. He would show automated slide presentations and pushed for professionalizing the campaign using computers. Ted enjoyed this job. He was there the full three months.

Ted said his goal was to graduate from law school so he had better get on with it. He was scheduled to go to the University of Utah in the fall of 1973, but decided at the last minute not to attend. He wrote them and told them he had been in an accident and had to cancel his coursework for that fall. He went to the University of Puget Sound instead because he didn't want to leave the state.

He and Liz were still together but he didn't see her as much because he was too busy "running around the state." He said he had no interest in other girls.

A woman who was one of Liz's friends said of Ted,

> Ted was spaced out on several occasions. One night he was walking to his home and me and Liz passed him on the sidewalk. He didn't even recognize Liz, who at the time was his girlfriend. I have seen him spaced out many times. His response to anxiety was to space out.

Another woman said that Ted was a loner. She added,

> If he couldn't find his girlfriend, he would call around with a panic feeling. One night he couldn't find Liz and he sat in a bar for hours talking to me about it. He didn't seem normal. He tied Liz down for sex. He was brilliant, outgoing, pretentious, and very deceiving.

It was clear that by the fall of 1972 Ted had serious emotional problems but wasn't getting any help for them. Through the spring of 1973 he had employment but still nothing he was satisfied with. He had serious sexual problems that would not go away on their own. If he was arrested on a sex charge it would ruin his career and he would feel severe humiliation. It's possible that he thought of his mother and what she went through when she was pregnant with him. It would be less than a year before girls would begin disappearing in Washington. I felt fairly certain that Ted Bundy had killed them. Could he sense that he was getting to that point? If so, what would he do to attempt to maintain control over himself?

EIGHTEEN

Return of Marjorie

Ted said that during the summer of 1973 he became restless so he decided to take a short vacation and also to do some research on polling through the telephone. He went to San Francisco and contacted Marjorie. Since Ted was so often not truthful about his motivations, I felt I had to read between the lines. Did he just happen to go to San Francisco to do this research or was his primary motivation to see Marjorie? I assumed it was the latter. What was he really after?

Ted and Marjorie went to dinner and it was enjoyable. He stayed at a motel for the first couple of nights and then was invited to stay at Marjorie's apartment. He was there for about a week. Marjorie had said that when they broke up several years ago, they had continued to talk on the phone so him showing up wasn't totally unexpected.

They talked things over and decided to consider the possibility of reestablishing their relationship. It was decided that she would come up to Seattle in September and they would continue to consider the possibility of getting back together. Ted would get permission to use a friend's condo at a ski resort.

Meanwhile, in the fall of 1973, Ted had been accepted to work on his law degree at the University of Puget Sound. He was still with Liz and he was making promises that he would marry her when he earned his law degree and got established in a career. He didn't tell her about having spent a week with Marjorie in San Francisco or about his plans to meet with her in Seattle. It appears that Ted was wife shopping in an attempt to find someone who would make a good impression on others when he settled on a career. Perhaps he thought he could resolve his sexual problems if he was a politician and had a beautiful wife at his side. He felt that Marjorie would likely make a better wife for a politician than would Liz.

Marjorie came up and they spent time together.

It went well so they made plans to get together for the Christmas holidays. Ted didn't tell Liz about this. When the time came, Ted borrowed a friend's condo at a ski resort and he and Marjorie spent their time skiing, talking about their future together, having sex—which represented a significant change in the nature of their relationship—and generally enjoying each other's company. Liz and her daughter were in Utah spending the holidays with her parents. It was likely that Ted had told her that he needed to stay in Seattle to catch up on his law studies.

Marjorie was satisfied with being with Ted during the Christmas holidays, but Ted wasn't. A proposal for marriage was made but it's unclear who suggested it first. When Marjorie got on the plane to return to San Francisco, she went with a commitment from Ted that they would be getting married by spring. But again, Ted couldn't handle it. Ted hurried back to Liz, who had returned from her trip to Utah. Ted said,

> I felt bad about it. I thought, what am I trying to
> prove? Do I love Liz or Marjorie? [Marjorie] came up
> for the Christmas holidays. We talked about our
> future, even marriage. I believe she felt she was
> getting old and she pressed the issue of getting
> married. I felt terrible pangs of guilt because of Liz. It
> could have been ideal, but I didn't love Marjorie as
> much as I loved Liz.

His statement: "it could have been ideal" suggests that he was seeking an answer to something. During the summer of 1972, Ted had been sexually involved with a couple of other girls. His dissociation and aggressiveness during sex was frightening to them. His attempt to reconnect with Marjorie hadn't worked. I asked Ted what went wrong when he and Marjorie got together for the Christmas holidays.

> I was easygoing but I would forget things. I'd lock my
> keys in the car. Liz would accept it but Marjorie
> would go into a fit of rage. If I forget to get tomatoes
> at the store Liz would be okay with it but Marjorie
> would have a fit. She was more high-strung and
> impatient than Liz. On New Year's Day, Marjorie
> flew home with plans of marriage. I couldn't get in
> the car fast enough to get back to Liz.
> *How did you feel when you got back with Liz?*
> It was like a breath of fresh air. I had new feelings
> about her.
> *What did you do about Marjorie?*
> I couldn't bring myself to call and face her about the
> marriage plans.

So, what happened?
One Saturday Marjorie called and asked why I hadn't called or written. She was angry. I felt pretty casual. She said, "I never want to hear from you again" and she slammed the phone down. Marjorie said *she* broke off our relationship. I can't understand how information gets garbled.

Marjorie had a different version of the story. During my phone call to her I asked,

Ted said the two of you broke up but then you got back together later on in 1973. You originally broke up because of his inadequacies. What was there about him that made you consider getting back together with him?
He changed. He turned and went 180 degrees and all of a sudden—and this took place over a fair number of years—he got some jobs and he was in some political environments which brought money, a little bit of money, and he traveled and experienced people in situations in which he developed confidence.
But it was still a nervous type of confidence, sort of erratic. Then he started getting much more confident in his own environment, having contact with people I didn't like.
What do you mean by a nervous or erratic sense of confidence?
God, he was evasive! That's the best description of Ted, evasive. He could have been living three lives and I wouldn't have known it. I never really knew

exactly where he was or what he was doing, even if I asked him.

He was odd to begin with. He would pop up all the time in weird places. When I was down here in San Francisco he would just show up. When we were in Seattle he would just show up on the street. One day I walked out of my office at work at five o'clock and somebody said, "Hi Marjorie," and there he was. It was sort of a weird feeling. It wasn't like, "Hey, I rolled in today" or "I got down this way" or "I hitchhiked," or whatever. It was sort of like here he was. Sometimes I felt like he was watching me when he was not even around.

Then he got very weird. There was a weekend I went up there. This would have been in the fall of 1973. We were sitting in a restaurant and Ted was against women's lib and against abortion. He got real mean about it.

He was against an abortion law. He was very rigid about it. I couldn't believe it. I don't know if he was trying to be impressive or what.

He said you and he were engaged at one time.

Oh God, I guess so. Yeah, I guess that was true. Apparently at the same time he was planning to marry Liz.

Why do you think he would become engaged to you when he was with her?

After it all blew up, I gave it a lot of thought. I feel the reason he did that was to get back at me, to be vindictive. I suppose I really hurt him when I cut off the relationship many years ago.

He called me once [in the summer of 1973] and came down here to visit me. He was on a business

> trip, but even this seemed weird. I didn't even trust
> that he was really being put up by the Republican
> Committee in a hotel down here in San Francisco
> and being paid for it. I was that leery of him.
> He stayed with me that weekend and we sort of got
> back together again. And I said I would come up and
> see him and I did. They were very short weekends
> and this was the weekend he took me away to a
> cabin. It just wasn't terribly fruitful and I sort of felt
> he didn't like me anymore but I guess I just
> pushed it.

She said that when she first began dating Ted, he was easy to communicate with but "... now he wasn't interested one damn bit. It was just sort of weird and I didn't understand it." She felt that Ted was bored with her.

> And the second time I came up we had this lengthy
> discussion about where we were going to live. I was
> going to come up and find a place for me to live and
> we would get married. It was his first year of law
> school. I would pay for the rest of his law school. I
> had some money saved.
> And we talked about children and all sorts of things.
> And at first it seemed all right. However, I really
> didn't feel a lot of satisfaction about our plans. I came
> back home expecting to hear from him. He didn't
> call. I wrote him a couple of letters and I really laid
> out some feelings I had but he never answered them.

She called Ted in an attempt to understand what was going on. He had nothing to say and "… I realized I was talking to a wall." She said, "… he didn't have *any* answers. He didn't care. That's when I believed it was vindictive."

> I couldn't believe he was so insane to carry it through. What was he going to do if I really did show up there to get married?

NINETEEN

Spring 1974. End of UPS

Ted said, "Winter and spring were uneventful." But then he began to reveal that everything was not going well. Previously, he would tell me of a negative event and then he would attempt to undo the impact of his statement by expressing a positive outcome for that event. This time he began with a relatively positive statement and then immediately began undoing it.

He said he continued with his studies at University of Puget Sound (UPS) in the spring but they didn't go well.

> I was not content with the legal education at UPS. The night program was just not taking hold for me. I reapplied to the University of Utah Law School because it was just not becoming a productive year for me. I had a disagreement with a professor over a paper I had turned in and I wasn't going to get credit for it. I had missed a few classes. I withdrew from UPS without taking the final exams. It was probably test anxiety.

. . .

I could see it was clearly not test anxiety! In the fall of 1973 Ted's classes were going all right, but now in the spring of 1974 they weren't. It was the same pattern again and again. He would reach out for something he hoped would give him meaning and security but his hand always came back empty. Still, he did have employment. He said he got a job preparing a biannual budget for the Department of Emergency Services and commuted from Seattle to Olympia. The job was enjoyable because he had some responsibility for the budget. A close friend to the governor had gotten him the job. His next plan, however, was to go to the University of Utah Law School and get a law degree. Would this be another desperate attempt to resolve his problems?

The Raft Trip

There was one significant event that occurred during the summer of 1974 that convinced me of Ted's violent nature. This information came from Dick Larsen, Associate Editor of the Seattle Times, and Larry Voschall, a reporter tor the Times.

Ted and his date, a girl named Becky, along with Larry and his date, Susan, were to take a leisurely run down the Yakima River. The trip was to go like this: They would take two cars to the river. Ted's car would be parked downstream at a spot where they planned to exit the river. They would drive Larry's car with the raft seven miles upstream where the four of them would inflate the six-man raft and enter the river. They would float down the river to where Ted's car was parked and someone would drive with Ted in his car back upstream to Larry's car. They would return and pick up the raft and Larry and Susan and return to Seattle. The river was fairly wide and while there were a few rough places they anticipated no problems because they would be floating on the smooth side of the river. This was particularly important because Becky could not swim.

Larry told me in a telephone conversation,

> The thing about this raft trip is I had always seen Ted as a gentleman's gentleman, rather suave, the type of person that would never step out of line. As the raft trip progressed his personality went from that to a type of personality that none of us really wanted anything to do with. As a matter of fact, I don't think I've seen Ted since. That was about two years ago this summer. At any rate, there was one incident where Becky was in an inner tube tied on to the raft and he untied her halter top and let it fall away. It was an embarrassment to her. It was clearly out of character with his personality.
>
> But more than that, we got in a couple of really tight situations which were very unpleasant. He put his head under a waterfall and almost overturned the raft. Becky almost went under. He just seemed to enjoy seeing people frightened. As the trip progressed, we went over a waterfall. [At one-point Ted let Becky drift in the inner tube over to the waterfall knowing she couldn't swim.]
> Then he got in the inner tube and cut himself loose and floated by himself for a while. He decided he was tired of us and went down ahead of us in the river. When we got down to where the car was, he went up to pick up the other car. It was only about seven miles and it took him a long time to come back.

His personality went from a very pleasant person to someone who was practically unbearable to be with. I don't know whether he was tired of his amateur partners or what, but it was one of the most unusual personality transformations I've seen. I've been a reporter for about ten years and it's one of the strangest things I've seen. I believe he's got a split personality, a dual personality.

It was so strange because he was the kind of person who would come to a party and he was so intelligent and he could easily carry on a conversation and he was so polite. Then to see the other side of him was so shocking. His two personalities were so different that after that the three of us really didn't want anything to do with him.

Was there any other time when you saw this change in his personality?

I really didn't. I had been to a few parties with him. I had the impression that he had a lot of money. He was always well groomed, good clothes, and very well-mannered. And that was what impressed me, to see a really different side to him. So, when all of this other stuff started coming up, I thought I needed to talk to the authorities so I gave them a call.

When Ted was arrested, he sent a letter to the Times in Seattle asking for financial assistance. It was of interest to Larry that Ted made no effort to say he was innocent. "He was asking for sympathy but making no effort to say 'I didn't do it. Help me out.'" Larry then continued talking about the river trip:

I don't know. It was a fascinating encounter, I'll tell you that. It was just that personality change. In spite of all our objections he really put us in a couple of tight spots where somebody could have got hurt. Going through the turbulence where the waterfall came out into the river, we almost lost the raft. There was no reason to go over to that part at all. We had a half mile wide river and much of it was very smooth.
Do you have any idea why he untied Becky's halter?
No, that has always seemed to be a real strange thing. I don't think I was initially looking in that direction. Then I turned and I saw the halter fall. She was a very proper gal. That surprised me. I've taken other trips where that happened and we didn't think anything of it, but with his personality and with Becky it seemed very strange.
Had he dated her much?
I don't think more than a couple times. That night after he finally came back, we headed back to Seattle, about a two-hour trip. We wanted to stop to get something to eat. He didn't want to and he wasn't talking to anybody. Becky said it probably was because he didn't have any money with him. Becky said she'd buy. God, he didn't say a word! When he's talkative he's very talkative. I always thought that something happened in that hour and a half when he was gone. He was a completely different person.

A split or dual personality? This was similar to Kim's account of him during their lake trip in the summer of 1972. In particular, this is what Ted was like when they were driving the dirt roads in the Lake Sammamish area, but in the case of Kim, he was with only one person. In the river trip event there were three others, and one of them was a reporter.

My overall impression at this point of the assessment was that Ted had a very dark side to him and, instead of him improving his control over his emotions and behavior, he was getting worse. With Kim in the driving around the hills episode, Ted was able to regain his composure after he blew up at her. In the raft trip episode, he wasn't able to. He withdrew within himself and his behavior was inappropriate.

TWENTY

The Salt Lake Period

Liz went to Salt Lake towards the end of the summer in 1974 and got an apartment for Ted in the Avenues, an older section of Salt Lake located east of the capitol building. She returned to Seattle where she continued to stay. Ted moved down and began his classes at the law school.

He said,

> I had a difficult time adjusting to Salt Lake. Some of it was meeting new people. I began missing classes and by the middle of October I had stopped going to school altogether.
> *Why do you think that was?*
> I don't know why. I had invested money and savings to come down. I don't know why it was.
> *What did you do if you were not going to your classes?*
> I made bookshelves and I did some reading and the days flashed by. Around the 1st of December I went up and talked to my professors to see what I could do to stay in the program. They said if I could make up

my homework I could stay. In January of 1975, I was a regular in all my classes and I passed the courses and the year was salvaged. It restored my confidence. I called Liz three or four times a week. The phone bill was high so we talked about whether or not I should continue calling her.

Something was drastically wrong but Ted wouldn't talk about it. This was understandable because he was undergoing an evaluation which could have an effect on whether or not he would go to prison. Nevertheless, the pattern I was seeing was not one of an up-and-coming lawyer/politician with the world ahead of him. Even if Ted wasn't violent—which I was sincerely beginning to doubt—he was deeply troubled and clearly wasn't the person that his supporters believed him to be. It was clear that Ted had been successful in one thing: convincing his supporters of his potential. It must have been devastating to him to miss opportunity after opportunity in his life, and never deliver on his dreams. Ted Bundy was not the man he wanted everyone to believe he was. What else was he hiding?

When he went to summer school at Stanford University in 1967, he was very excited about the program. He enjoyed his professors and the lectures and his dream was to work for the government or in some way to help the poor. But then, he was deeply in love with Marjorie and believed they would have a good life together. His future was ahead of him.

Now, he was in Salt Lake, he was enrolled in law school but he couldn't bring himself to go to the classes. He was still planning something with Liz, but she wasn't with him so he couldn't go to her apartment when he needed to be with someone. Things were not going well for him.

Before coming to the 90-Day Evaluation Unit, Ted had indicated to the authorities that he and Liz were planning to get married. I think he felt that if he was getting married it might help allay suspicions that he was a killer. I don't believe that he was simply using Liz. He went out with some girls in Salt Lake and he talked with some of them about Liz. I believe that he was emotionally dependent on her yet couldn't marry her.

Ted continued his classes in the spring of 1975 and went to summer school. By the time fall came he was again excited about going to school. He had made friends and had been going out with three or four girls in Salt Lake City, reassuring himself that these were only friendships. However, I talked to a couple of girls that he went out with. They talked about a sexual relationship they had with him.

I spoke to a mother of one of these girls. She said,

My first impression of him was that he was good looking and he was charming. He took my daughter out a couple of times in November 1974 [coincidentally, around the same time of the attempted kidnapping of Carol DaRonch] and then he disappeared and I didn't see him until the following spring. Then one day he dropped by my apartment on his bicycle, casually, like nothing had happened.

In July of 1975, I put on a going away party for my daughter, Judy [pseudonym]. She was a good cook and she would circulate around and talk to all the guests. That night they stayed up all night. Ted got cozy with Judy's friend Tasha [pseudonym]. When Judy went back east Bundy dated Tasha for about a week. Then all of a sudden nothing. It was just like with Judy.

> Tasha came up one night and said, "I don't understand Bundy." I said, "There's something strange about him. You can never get close to that boy. He's nice but he's not warm."
>
> Tasha said she tried and tried to talk to him about his past and what his childhood was like but he never would. We tried to psych him out, wondering what in the world it was with him. Tasha said Ted would ride his bicycle around Murray Park a lot. That's a long way from his apartment. Tasha had gotten quite intimate with him. Both Tasha and Judy thought a relationship was beginning to develop, but then after a few dates he just dropped out of sight.
>
> I'm a person who likes to put my arms around people and when I put my arms around Bundy, he just wasn't warm.

The summer and fall of 1975 were very stressful for Ted. In late June, Ted met a 31-year-old single mother. He seemed to be fairly sociable but somewhat aloof. She began dating him and at times they would go on outings. Ted always allowed her seven-year-old son to be with them. He began drinking more heavily and on one occasion he passed out drunk in her apartment. She told Don Hull, the presentence investigator, that he frequently talked to her about his girlfriend Liz and how she had lost respect for him because he dated other girls while being engaged to her. He talked about his political aspirations to someday be governor of Washington. He told her his world was falling apart. She broke off their relationship because he was becoming increasingly moody and erratic in his behavior.

Ted was reaching out for something that summer but he

wasn't finding it. It appeared that he might have come to Utah not only to pursue a law degree but perhaps to find a new beginning. If so, he wasn't finding it. His life was seriously deteriorating.

One woman I talked to in Salt Lake said he was always polite around women, he was always immaculate, he was very outgoing, he was always in control, he rarely seemed bitter or depressed, and he had a good sense of humor. Importantly, he felt there was no difference between right or wrong. Ted came to her house on one occasion and parked in front for five minutes before coming in. She observed him out her window. His chest and shoulders were heaving. When he came in, he denied there was anything wrong.

The picture I was getting of Ted Bundy did not add up to a well-adjusted, charming social climber who would one day be the governor of Washington. There was no question in my mind that his successful persona was just a cover for a very disturbed young man. And, by this point, I had reason to believe that he did indeed have the capacity for extreme anger and violence.

TWENTY-ONE

Getting Religious

Ted said he typically gravitated toward a strong counter-culture element of society. However, in November of 1974, he was introduced to The Church of Jesus Christ of Latter-day Saints (LDS), commonly known as the Mormons. He invited the LDS missionaries to visit him. He took the missionary discussions for two or three months and he attended the LDS branch near the University of Utah campus. He decided not to continue with it at that time but in July or the beginning of August of 1975, he again decided to become involved with it. Liz was a member of the Church but she was inactive. As to why he was interested in the Church, he said:

> I got tired of my own failures and I wanted to adapt a more disciplined approach. I felt my lifestyle could be improved. I felt there was joy and warmth of fraternity within the church. It was a church of the people, owned and operated by the people.
> *What were you seeking?*

> Oh, maybe, like when one sees a painting and you want it because it represents something that you want to be part of.
> *But Ted, you were smoking and drinking then. You didn't stop before getting baptized into the church.*
> I felt I could get the strength to stop smoking and drinking after joining the church.

If he felt he could only get the strength to stop smoking and drinking after joining the Church, did he mean he hoped it might also help him control his violent nature? Ted told me he had never had an interest in religion, and in particular he had no interest in the LDS Church. Yet, here he was telling me that he had been in Salt Lake for only a few months and began exploring the Church. The LDS missionaries who taught him about the Church said he seemed sincere. They met with him not just once but for a series of discussions, and he went to church at least a few times.

Ted did not strike me as a person who could be easily talked into something, especially into joining a church. He was lying to them about his smoking and drinking, but he appeared sincere when he talked to the missionaries. Why would he want to join the Church?

On November 8, 1974, he attempted to kidnap Carol DaRonch, and he was suspected of kidnapping and killing Debby Kent on that same night, though without a conviction I couldn't use that in the evaluation. One would expect that when Carol was able to escape from his car and get away it would frighten him since she could identify him. He now had a victim who was still alive. If he had killed Debby Kent, the only reason I could imagine him taking that kind of risk was if his need for a victim was completely out of his control. If all of this was true, it's understandable why he would suddenly show an interest in God. And it could have been with a religion other than the Mormons. It just happened to be that the people he was beginning to associate with when he was in Salt Lake were LDS.

But, is it possible that Ted really *was* interested in religion? Was he becoming anxious about his soul and about his sins? Considering that he had already expressed his indifference for the concepts of right and wrong, did he even believe that killing someone was a sin? Did he fear punishment from God? I had the following conversation with him about this:

Ted, what is anxiety like for you?
I don't waste emotional energy or weaken myself by letting small matters bother me. Law school may have caused some anxiety but I don't get nervous without a cause. To stay level headed and rational is important.

What's your philosophy of life?
I'm not sure if there is any brief way to summarize it.
I remember trying to come up with one not long ago.
I've come up with a hundred speeches for Judge
Hansen.
Man is an arrogant creature, believing he can control the universe. If you get in a jet you see how insignificant you are.
What's your belief about happiness and love?
I should be able to live my life to the degree it doesn't

interfere with others. I believe in non-violence. I'm opposed to the Vietnam War. I want gun control.
Have you ever been violent?
I struck Liz only once and it was lightly when she was hysterical.
What's your belief about death?
It's inevitable for each of us… I haven't had much experience with it. Presently, I don't fear death. I face it here at the prison. I don't fear anyone or anything. I have no belief in life after death. Life on the earth has purpose and meaning. If there is life after death you will live it and have a good one. If not, you will have fulfilled your purpose here.
What's your personal view of life after death?
I don't plan on it. If there is one okay, and if not, okay. My view of death is that the concept was created for security, to have a feeling of immortality. Heaven should be a pure intellectual existence. Heaven is an ideal material world as people see it. I believe heaven is a pure intellectual force where I can convene with others who have passed on. To become immortal and preserve one's soul is of lasting value. The forces guiding my destiny are not open to a rational approach. With what has happened, even though I am innocent, I don't feel that my word will be accepted in any way.

This suggests that Ted doesn't believe in a God who will punish a person for sins they have committed here on earth. To say that heaven is "a pure intellectual force where I can convene with others who have passed on" sounds like a group of people standing around discussing philosophical issues.

It's clear then that Ted showed an initial interest in becoming religious in November of 1974, telling the missionaries that he had a belief in God. Then he decided not to become a member of the Church. I believe that when he wasn't immediately caught and arrested for the DaRonch or the Kent crimes he felt an egotistical pride because he had gotten away with it and didn't need religion any longer. It's as though he felt he had it under control (that is, he wouldn't get caught) so he didn't need a religion to help him gain that control.

However, in August 1975, he again got active in the Church and was baptized. Within a couple of weeks, he was arrested by Sergeant Bob Hayward of the Utah Highway Patrol.

TWENTY-TWO

Thematic Apperception Test

The Thematic Apperception Test, commonly known simply as the TAT, is a projective personality test comprised of a number of black and white pictures of various situations, most of them of people interacting in some manner. A person taking the test is asked to make up stories for the pictures. The TAT is a "projective test" because when a person tells a story to match a picture, he "projects" aspects of himself into the picture. He is saying something about himself through the story. An analysis of a set of stories reveals information about a person's motives, fears, hopes, and anticipations.

It was clear at this point of the evaluation that Ted had some serious emotional problems. I wanted to see what a projective test would tell me about the inner workings of Ted Bundy.

I'm putting the stories and my suggested interpretation of the stories in this chapter for historical reasons. The interpretations of the stories are my own.

There are multiple ways to consider each story and you may want to devise your own. Where necessary I have given a brief description of the picture Ted was looking at when he told his story. The pictures are copyrighted and publication of them is illegal so I can't include the images here.

NAME: Theodore Bundy
DATE: April 28, 1976

Picture number 1: A boy sitting at a table looking at a violin. There is a white object under the violin which appears to be sheet music.

> This is a young man who has been practicing all afternoon on his violin. He looks tired if not sleepy. He's been at school all day and has been up since early in the morning and came home and practiced his violin and has set it down now and appears to be so sleepy that he's about ready to nod off. To me there appears to be an element of being tired on his face, which could also be boredom, but he looks like the kind that would faithfully practice his violin because he looks like the kind of boy who would want to learn how to play it. I suppose he's just about finished because when you're so tired you can't… he couldn't practice anymore anyway, but he'll keep at it because it's important to him and it's important to those around him.

Interpretation: Ted has been struggling with his legal problems since he was first arrested on the evening of August 16th, 1975. Also, Ted was struggling with his attempt to get through college with a law degree. The boy in the picture is about to give up because he's too worn out to continue, but "it's important to him and it's important to those around him," so he won't stop.

Theme: You can't give up no matter how tired you get.

Picture number 2: (His story describes the picture.)

> This is a family, a father, a mother leaning on the tree, the father tilling the fields in the springtime, a young daughter whose interests are not in the fields and not in a family life on the farm, but perhaps in the city with another occupation: being a teacher or a nurse or a doctor. She's pained inside because she doesn't want to leave her parents, but she knows that she must find her own life and she's trying to think of the best way to initiate the subject of her leaving with them. She has a feeling that they wouldn't agree with her, or they would try to convince her to stay, which would hurt her very much because she wouldn't want to go against their wishes and yet eventually she does talk to them and finds to her surprise that they know that she is looking for something else and to find a place for her in the city with relatives so that she can attend school.

Interpretation: He is identifying with the girl in this picture. The girl is not interested in "the family life on the farm." Ted wanted a career that was different from family tradition. Also, he was not satisfied that Liz was good enough to be a politician's wife. He was always seeking someone different. He was never able to stay with jobs, schools, or other relationships. The "farm life" is not spectacular enough for him. He has always been looking for something elsewhere to satisfy him but has failed. He has to keep looking. The "family" in this story could be his mother, his girlfriend Liz, Marjorie, or anyone who have attempted to satisfy him. They all realize that he has to make his own decisions but there is nothing in the story that says they are happy about it.

Theme: One has to look somewhere else other than where he is to find satisfaction.

Picture number 3: Woman sitting with her head down on a seat. She could be crying or is simply tired. There is a small object beside her.

> Here is a woman who is very distraught or at least appears resigned and tired. She has a gun that lays on the floor, which she dropped there in utter defeat, so as it were, knowing that death was not the answer but very frustrated about living. Perhaps realizing in her own mind that because her husband left, because things seem hard was not a reason to give up and that she still has her family to think of. She may fall asleep there and wake up later and maybe even wonder what drove her to such lengths to… what made her so unhappy with herself or life to want to go so far. She'll go on living and it won't be easy but she'll pick up that gun and throw it away and do the best she can.

Interpretation 1: Ted was frustrated with the way life had turned out for him up to this point. He had achieved only a taste of success in a career. Relationships have not worked out for him. Now he is in prison. He won't give up but from here on it won't be easy.

Interpretation 2: There's another possibility. *If* Ted had killed several women and *if* he was unable to stop, he could feel defeated and totally worn out and "unhappy with [himself] or with life." Perhaps he has considered suicide.

Theme: Life is extremely troubling but you can't give up no matter how much you want to.

Picture number 4: A man and a woman. She is holding on to him and he is pulling away from her. He has an intense look on his face. In the background off to the side is a picture of a woman with bare legs showing.

> Both of them have interesting expressions on their faces. The one of the woman is of admiration almost, and of passion. The look on the man's face is one where he looks eager and confident. He may be leaving for some—for a trip or an adventure and she, proud of what he is about to do, wants to kiss him one more time before he leaves. He is dressed in the shirt of a working man but may not have his tie on. They're married and they haven't been married long, but she appears to be very much in love with him and he appears very eager to do what he has to do. It ends up that he was prepared for what he had to do because he had that confidence and he was ready and he came back and now with that job off his mind, he could turn to her and have the same love in his eyes that she has for him.

Interpretation: He sees a couple who have been married only a short time. She is very much in love with him and she is trying to hold on to him. He, however, can't return that passion towards her. There is something that he has to do before he can reciprocate her love. He is eager (driven) and he is confident (he is skilled in doing it). Only after he does what he has to do and has satisfied that unmentioned need can he turn his attention to his wife and her needs. This suggests something that has become an obsession and a compulsive drive for Ted and he has to give in to it. Only after he has achieved what he has to do can he stop thinking about it. When he has done "the job" he can once again "have the same love in his eyes that she has for him." This is similar to Kim reporting that Ted couldn't stop driving in the back areas of Lake Sammamish, looking for something and not being able to settle down until he found it.

Theme: There are some needs that are more necessary than being home with his passionate wife. My take on it is that he is speaking of his drive to find victims.

Picture number 5: An elderly woman is standing by a window but she is looking straight ahead rather than out the window. A younger man with a shirt and tie and a coat is holding onto his hat. He is looking down rather than at the woman.

> The woman in the picture is the man's mother. She is an older woman in her 60s. The man has just returned home to find that his father has just died. She has cried all her tears. There is very little she can do. She has been ready and prepared for this and he, younger and not quite prepared, is taking it very much harder than she. It is difficult for them both, but because he came to her, they'll both gain—they'll both be able to support each other and make the initial separation easier than it would have been otherwise. I suppose I would hope that he would ask her to come live with his family because she would be

alone—all the children have moved away. And she will.

Interpretation: This may be about him being born illegitimate. His mother had several months to prepare herself for his birth after she was deserted by Ted's father. Ted wasn't informed about it and so he wasn't prepared for it when he did learn about it as a teenager. He is taking it very hard [which he did] but if he comes to her about it, both can gain from it.

Theme: The loss of a father is difficult. He needs to take care of his mother.

Picture number 6: An elderly man is talking to a younger man. The older man is leaning towards the younger man. The younger man is staring off in space as he appears to be listening. The younger man appears to be afraid.

> Two attorneys at a friend's table—well actually it looks more like an attorney and a client. The attorney being the gentleman with the mustache, the light hair, dark suit; the client dark hair, younger, light suit. They have just heard testimony from a damaging witness and the attorney is about to whisper to his client to take it easy, that it's not as bad as it sounds, to try to comfort him to try to calm him down. The young man appears bitter like an accomplice has testified against him or like a friend who said something that hurt him very deeply but also angered him. And yet he has restrained himself. So, his attorney tells him this and he tries to understand, although he can't fully, but he trusts his attorney and this makes it easier for him. He is definitely found

innocent in my stories. There is no doubt about it.
Yes, well the attorney looks like a good one, but looks
are deceiving. There can be no happier ending.

Interpretation: This one is fairly easy to interpret. Ted had a good defense attorney who likely tried to encourage him by telling him that it wasn't as bleak as it appeared. Who was the friend who said something that hurt and angered him? Ted came to the attention of the police when his girlfriend Liz informed them that her boyfriend Ted might be the person they were looking for. There were a couple of others who knew Ted fairly well and were friends with him who called the police on him.

Theme: People he has trusted have turned against him and he's not fully certain that he can even trust his attorney. The more general theme is that one can't really trust anyone.

Picture number 7: A young boy by what appears to be a cabin. The door is open and it's dark inside. The boy is sitting on the landing in what appears to be overalls. He has bare feet and he seems to be daydreaming.

> He's a little boy that lives in the neighborhood of an old pioneer fort and on bright school days finds it great entertainment to go and sit in the old log cabins and watch the tourists who pay to see what he can see every day. He loves going there because that is part of summer. I thought he was eating something, but he doesn't have anything. He just sits there and watches the tourists come from California and New Jersey and points all across the United States to his hometown to see a fort which is to him just like home. He comes there every day and tells them stories about

the fort that he has heard from his parents and is
really quite a curiosity for the tourists, and he enjoys
it and loves this strange old place which is so rich in
stories, and will come there nearly every day that
summer to be an unofficial guide with the people.

Interpretation: Ted seemed to enjoy telling me about the time when he was a child and he had two friends he had fun with. He called the three of them the "three musketeers." That seemed to be an adventurous and fun time in his life.

Theme: The memories of the freedom and friends he had as a child were wonderful. In the story, the boy is an important authority. It's a story of freedom and nostalgia.

Picture number 8: This entire picture is dark other than a man who appears to be looking out an open window. It's light outside and he is silhouetted against the light as if he is about to climb out.

A man staring out of an open window. It is difficult
for me to tell anything more about him or about
what his expression is or what the room is like. It is
an entirely dark picture. Sometimes it reminds me of
staring out my window or the windows of the prison
looking at the freeway, but there are no bars there so
it can't be that. He's looking out across the view he
has from his upstairs window. It's been a long hot
summer day. He has opened the window to cool off
his apartment. The sun is very, very low in the sky
and yet he sees a brilliant sunset which he always
enjoys watching when one can be seen. He'll stand
there by the window with the cool air rushing in
until his apartment is cooled and the sun is set and

he can rest in comfort in his apartment. The man is staring, not looking out his window, suggesting a strong desire to be out there. Normally he could walk out the door and be away from the heat, but something is preventing him from doing so.

Interpretation: This could be referring to being in prison. There are no bars on his window in this story yet it reminds him of looking out the prison window at the freeway. It's a dark picture as Ted sees it. He can open his window but something has to happen from the outside ("cool air rushing in") that gives him the rest and comfort he is seeking. There are a number of possibilities as to what the "cool air" might be referring to. It's dark inside but beautiful and refreshing outside. When the sun goes down it will be dark inside but that's all right now that something from the outside has comforted him.

Theme: It's been a long hot summer day (his legal problems) but he can see that which created the heat turn into something beautiful—the sunset.

Picture number 9. Man in cemetery, looking down at a grave.

> There is a sinister gentleman standing in the middle of the graveyard, it would appear. In spite of his solid face and his rather bizarre dress, and even because it appears by the light it's late in the day and it's getting dark, he's come to pray for a child and lay flowers on the grave of a child who was his—who belonged to he and his wife before their divorce. People don't give him much credit for sentiment but underneath the rather evil, rather sinister, sad face, there is someone

who can feel a great deal of loss—and come late at night so people won't mock him so he can be alone in the quiet and think his own thoughts. Perhaps it's because he doesn't want to show the goodness that is inside of him and reveal the weakness (which he thinks is a weakness) that he has for sorrow and sadness. He comes there once a week, stops and thinks about the life he could have had but he knows it is long past time for that life as long as it has passed, and yet he still cares very much and only wishes that things had been different.

Interpretation: This one is especially interesting. The combination of the words "sinister" and "gentleman" suggests a person who has two sides to his personality—one menacing (sinister) and the other an aristocrat (gentleman). Ted was a killer who wanted people to see him as an up and coming politician.

Who is the child? Is he referring to the abortion Liz had? Or, could he possibly be referring to himself as an illegitimate child? Or still, could it be Ann Burr, the girl who went missing (and who Ted was suspected of killing) when he was a teenager? Regardless, he is feeling a deep loss of the child.

There are two strong themes in the story. One theme is that the person is seen as evil by others but there is goodness and the capability for sorrow in him.

Another major theme is that the person feels bad about his life and wishes it could have been different.

But it's too late.

Theme: Even an evil person can feel sorrow and wish that things had been different.

. . .

Picture number 10: Woman standing on a bridge looking down into the water.

> This scene is a scene along a riverbank in France. It's one of those large commercial rivers that's there to transport the produce—the vegetables, goods of France. It's in France's internal regions, a bridge over the river meant routinely for unloading sacks of potatoes from a barge to a large storage mill. And on that bridge over the river quietly, mid-day, a woman stands to watch the river, contemplating her own life during her lunch hour. She is thinking of the many thoughts that one thinks when one sees a river run by: the places that it goes to, the fun—the good times that have been had with other people. It's like a stream of thought. She remembers, with happiness and some sadness, the people she has known and looks forward with some expectation but has some indecision about the future. She's lonely, but only because the person she wants to be with is not there to be with her. But he will return. She comes here each day because it's the kind of place she can stand to think and deal with her thoughts and feel relaxed.

Interpretations: Ted has conflicting feelings of happy memories but he's not part of it. In the TAT a person can speak of himself whether the picture is of a man or a woman. In this picture, Ted is standing off to the side watching progress occur but he's not part of it. He's thinking about happy memories but with some sadness. He's looking forward to the future with some indecision. He's lonely because the person he wants to be with (Liz?) is not there. However, he will return to her.

Theme: Wishing for something he once had but doesn't

have now and isn't sure about the decisions he will have to make in the future.

Picture number 11: Woman looking in the door of a room.

> The young woman is obviously crying or in some sort of pain. She's holding her head, her face that is. It's hard to understand just why it is that she feels that way. She's received some news and is very startled by it. Her son it seems was killed in a bicycle accident with a car and she was in another room and just came into this room and is holding the door open, but is unable to go any further. Her grief is too great. She can't think. She can only cry and let emotion take its course. But she is a young mother and she'll have more children and one that will compensate. Her grief will certainly diminish, but she will always remember her son and will always be very fond of him because he was her first.

Interpretation: Ted seems to be talking about the grief his mother is feeling over him. After all, he was her first. There's a finality to it. Her son is dead, not just injured. His career has ended.

Theme: Mother grieves over a permanent loss of her first-born son.

Picture number 12: House in snowstorm.

> It's a small mountain village—either some remote section of the Alps where each winter the snows pile high and the small village cottages become covered

and overcome, drifted in snow. It's snowing, so apparently the weather is quite fierce even now, as the snowdrifts indicate. But inside it looks warm as the glow around the windows seems to be light inside. It may even be Christmas although I can't tell. It looks like some of the windows are decorated. It's always nice to celebrate Christmas under these conditions because it makes being together and it makes home all that much warmer and all that much more secure when the weather outside is so threatening and so fierce. It looks like the storm is raging still by the way the clouds have gathered in the distance, but there's nothing better than being inside on a night like this. Reminds me of a house that some skiing directors, friends of mine have. They have a very comfortable cabin in Park City. It's always nice to go inside from outside.

Interpretation: He's talking about his current circumstances where he's facing being put in prison and the loss of his future. It's "threatening and fierce" and "the storm is raging still." How nice it would be to be away from the storm, in a comfortable cabin, where there are friends, happiness, and it's "secure." Christmastime is a time when love and companionship is particularly enjoyable.

Theme: He needs a place where he can get away from the fierce storm going on around him. A place where he can be accepted by friends. The violent storm is still going on and he is out in it.

MAKE UP PICTURE: In this one, the person is handed a blank card and is asked to make up a picture and then tell a story to it.

Well, the picture that's in my mind the most—all the time--is a picture of a girl I love very much. It's a picture of her apartment and the memories of us being together. But the one that occurs most often in my mind is the picture of her kneeling, cleaning the oven. Just standing there in the doorway watching her clean the oven when she didn't know I was there, really marveling about how in spite of all the grease around her elbows, the smudges on her face, that I really cared for her--knowing that I could take her any way she was, dirty or clean or any way. In that picture of her when I came over to her, and how happy we were to see each other. And I only hope I know how it ends.

Interpretation: There appears to be two things going on here. First, Ted is aware of the purpose of this test and what it is that I'm trying to discover about him, so he's trying to tell me how much he loves Liz. It's the same as telling the police and others that he and Liz are engaged and will be getting married in December.

On one hand it's contrived, but I think not totally so. Ted had tears in his eyes when he told this story. It indicates that the girl in the picture, whom he suggests is Liz, is someone the man in the picture—Ted—is deeply in love with. In the picture, he is separated from her—he sees her in her home but he isn't there. He's been off somewhere and he's coming home.

Unlike his statements about Liz not being a politician's wife type of person, he is now willing to accept her with all her faults. In this picture, Liz is working hard to take care of the home. It's interesting that he puts the next to the last sentence in the past tense: "When I *came* over to her…" and "… how happy we *were* to see each other." His last statement that "… I only hope I know how it ends" is a deep desire for this reunion. I felt his tears were genuine and not a manipulation to make me feel sorry for him.

Theme: He longs to be back with Liz and he is willing to accept her the way she is. He recognizes how much effort she puts into making a home and right now he really needs her.

Overall, these tests reveal deep emotions of longing, despair, death, discouragement, and hope. He needed Liz but it was often only when he was hurting.

TWENTY-THREE

Putting it All Together

"Do you think I killed those girls?"

Ted Bundy asked me this question after we had completed the final interview. We were standing in the corridor outside my office and Ted was about to return to his cell. It was an unusual question to ask since he had spent the past few weeks trying to convince me that he was completely innocent of having the intent or the behavior to hurt anyone. I was caught off guard by the question.

Did he really want an honest answer or was he trying to set me up for a rebuttal on my report in court should it be against him? If I said yes, he could argue in court that I was biased by the alleged crimes in Washington and therefore my report was not accurate. If I told him I didn't think he had killed any of the women in the northwest or in Utah he again would have a cause for a rebuttal saying that I had informed him in the corridor that I didn't think he was violent but then submitted a report to the court saying he was.

My assignment was to give my opinion about the nature of his personality not whether or not I thought he had killed anyone. With this question, Ted had put me in a lose-lose situation. My best option might have been to tell him that I couldn't, or wouldn't, answer his question. However, I said to him, "I don't know, but if you did, I believe you will do it again."

I'm sure it wasn't what he wanted to hear. He didn't say anything. He turned and walked back to his cell. In future conversations we had together he never again asked that question.

I had mixed feelings about why Ted had asked it. It was clear that he wanted to convince me that he was not violent. However, at times during the evaluation he seemed to want to talk beyond the requirements of the evaluation. Did he want to confess under conditions of confidentiality as one might do when talking to a priest? Was he carrying a heavy burden that he wanted to get rid of? But then, if he had been able to unload his burden, would it have made any difference to his personality or his behavior?

Likely not. When a person has a history of violence as did Ted, the memories and behavior patterns get buried so deep and become so entangled with normal memories and behaviors that any attempt to soften them would only be met with failure.

Dr. Van O. Austin, M.D., our prison psychiatrist, did a very thorough evaluation of Ted. He could find no signs of psychosis or of an organic brain disorder. He added,

A fourth diagnostic category which must be considered are the personality disorders (character disorders). These disorders are characterized by deeply ingrained, life-long, maladaptive behavior patterns.... He does have some features of the antisocial personality such as lack of guilt feelings, callousness, and a very pronounced tendency to compartmentalize and methodically rationalize his behavior. I feel that he also used this compartmentalization and rationalization in a passive and obstructive manner during my interviews. It is my impression that this is due to the deep-seated hostility which is evident on the psychological tests.....

In conclusion, I feel that Mr. Bundy is either a man who has no problems or is smart enough and clever enough to appear close to the edge of "normal." I do not feel that he is a candidate for treatment at this time. Since it has been determined by the court that he is not telling the truth regarding his present crime, I seriously question if he can be expected to tell the truth regarding participation in any program or probation agreement. It is my feeling that there is much more to his personality structure than either the psychologist or I have been able to determine. However, as long as he compartmentalizes, rationalizes and debates every facet of his life, I do not feel that I adequately know him, and until I do, I cannot predict his future behavior.

Mr. Donald G Morgan, MSW, who was then Supervisor and State Program Director at the Diagnostic Unit, gave a list of positives and negatives that were identified during Ted's time in the Diagnostic Program.

Positives:

1. The defendant has high intelligence.
2. It would appear from the social history that the defendant was not subject to severely

traumatizing influences in his childhood or adolescence.
3. Few or no distortions existed in the subject's relationship with his mother and stepfather.
4. From the information available, the developmental history shows no serious defects in physical development, habits, school adjustment, emotional maturation or sexual development.
5. From the available information, the defendant has adequate interests, hobbies and recreational pursuits.
6. From the available information, the defendant's habitual environmental pressures and responsibilities are average.
7. From the available information, it would appear that the defendant has had no previous attacks of emotional illness.
8. From the available information, the defendant has never received psychotherapy or counseling in the past.

Negatives:

1. The defendant has been convicted of a very serious charge where violence played a major role in the commission of the offense.
2. According to the psychological and psychiatric evaluations, when one attempts to understand Mr. Bundy, he becomes evasive.
3. Outwardly, the defendant appears confident and reveals himself as a secure person; underneath this veneer are fairly strong feelings of insecurity.

4. The defendant is somewhat threatened by people unless he feels he can structure the outcome of the relationship.
5. A fairly strong conflict was evidenced in the testing profile, that being the subject's fairly strong dependency on women, yet his need to be independent. Mr. Bundy would like a close relationship with females but is fearful of being hurt by them.
6. There were indications of general anger and more particularly well-masked anger toward women according to the psychological evaluation.
7. The defendant tends to remain emotionally distant from others probably as a defense against being hurt by them.
8. According to the psychological profile, the defendant has difficulty handling stress and has a strong tendency to run from his problems. His use of marijuana and the fact that he has been a heavy drinker at one time are indicators of difficulty in dealing with stress.
9. Passive/aggressive features were also evident. There was hostility observed on the subject's part which is directed toward the Diagnostic personnel even though Mr. Bundy would carefully point out that it is not aimed directly at those responsible for his evaluation.
10. The defendant has refused to acknowledge his guilt in the present offense. He maintains his innocence, therefore, making it impossible to consider a treatment program as Mr. Bundy indicates that he has no problems to treat. In the psychiatric evaluation, Dr. Van Austin states, "The second fact is that he adamantly denies his

guilt and in fact, denies that he has any personal problems of a magnitude that could lead to such a crime. I do not feel that he is a candidate for treatment at this time."

TWENTY-FOUR

Summary of the Findings

The information had been collected. The tests had been given, Ted had been interviewed multiple times and collateral contacts had been made to a number of people who were able to observe his behavior in different settings. Based on the combination of these I concluded the following:

Childhood

Ted had a lonely childhood. He was illegitimate, but while he was in Philadelphia, he had two aunts and grandparents who gave him love and attention that somewhat compensated for not having a father.

He wasn't yet five years old when he and his mother moved to Tacoma, Washington. The move was difficult for him. He lost the daily support from his aunts and grandparents so he clung to his mother. When she married John Bundy, Ted's name was changed for the third time: from Cowell to Nelson then to Bundy. When his mother had additional children, Ted was relegated to a lesser position in the family. To some extent, he was pushed aside for the new occupants who took his place. I found no evidence to suggest that Ted ever had an important place in the family. He was "just there," as one contact said.

The family was poor. Ted was shy and much of his enjoyment came from fantasy. He was intelligent but he didn't have many achievements in real life commensurate with his intellectual capabilities so his greatest achievements came from his daydreams.

Ted was passive. He was described as a follower rather than a leader. His fantasy life, which began with the weekly serials he listened to on the radio as a child, became a primary means of escape from his loneliness. However, rather than satisfying him, these fantasy activities only made him yearn for the real thing. His desire to become someone important was so strong that he memorized parts of political speeches he heard on the radio.

There were no indications of an open psychopathic process that was seen during his childhood. He wasn't cruel to animals, he didn't set fires, he didn't shoplift, and he was not rebellious. Again, he was a nice boy, a quiet boy, and seemingly a very normal boy who daydreamed about being a hero and a high achiever.

My conclusions regarding Ted Bundy's childhood were:

- He had an unfortunate childhood. His parents were not bad people but their time was taken up with their new family. Ted was displaced.
- Ted described his stepfather as a person who was always correcting him, not as a father who loved him. There was no father figure for him to talk to, play ball with, or go fishing with.

- Ted was shy as a child. If he received a lot of corrective type of communication from his parents it could generate a lack of self-worth. Too much correction often causes a child to rebel against it or to withdraw into a fantasy world where he can compensate by being a hero. Ted said he daydreamed of being adopted by Roy Rogers.
- Achievement was extremely important but he never attained it. To memorize parts of speeches of political leaders and to be humiliated because he wasn't in the top reading circle in the 4th grade reflects how emotionally hungry he was as a child.
- There were no indications that Ted was an angry child. He was obedient.
- The family was religious but there were no indications from Ted or from others who knew him that he ever had a strong belief in God.
- There were no indications from him that he had a family identity. This could make him hungry for a family when he became an adult. However, not having had the experience of being an included member of a family during his childhood could make it more difficult for him to have a natural feel for one later on.
- Overall, from what I learned about his childhood, I would expect Ted to have emotional problems later on. However, there were no signs to suggest that he would become a killer.

Teenage Years

Ted went to a junior high and high school where students from a poor area of the city were included with middle and upper middle-class students. He was a "nice guy" who didn't stand out. He was shy.

In his early teens, he had an interest in girls and in sports and he wanted to run for a class office in school. He went through puberty and developed a sexual drive resulting in him becoming interested in girls. The strength of his interest in sex and girlfriends was demonstrated by him saying he kissed and engaged in petting with girls.

Something happened when he was in junior high that must have been extremely traumatic. He stopped his relationships with girls. Ted never said what happened to cause him to do so, but whatever happened to scare him away from girls was powerful enough that he didn't go on any dates until he was a senior in high school, and even then, it was only to a school dance. A girl who knew him in junior high and high school said he was intelligent, good looking, and at least a few girls had a crush on him. He had a couple of friends. He went to school games but not to social activities. He was very shy. And very lonely.

A combination of intelligence and fantasy resulted in a powerful dream of going to college, finding a beautiful coed, and obtaining a career that would give him wealth and prestige. When he graduated from high school, he had the intelligence and a plan for his future but he didn't have the personality to go with it.

Cousin John's open plans for wealth and greatness in comparison to Ted's poverty and insignificance was a major issue.

I would expect that Ted developed a strong sexual appetite when he was in high school. The disappearance of Ann Marie Burr and Ted's insistence that he was unaware of it even though the entire city was traumatized by it suggests that he may have had something to do with it.

The trauma Ted experienced when his cousin John told him he was illegitimate was something he never got over. Ted told me it didn't bother him when his cousin John teased him about it but his girlfriends said he couldn't get over it. When Ted was a senior in high school and was invited by a few of the popular kids to go skiing with them it made him extremely happy. He was one of the boys when he was on the slopes. He was living the dream. It must have been a severe letdown when his friends went to parties and dances following a ski trip and Ted went home alone.

Ted likely had powerful sexual fantasies which may have been fueled by pornography. (I later learned that this was true.) The true crime magazines at that time had pictures of semi-nude girls on the covers. These were very popular back then, partly because of the stories and partly because of the covers.

Ted was likely developing psychopathic traits during his teens, but there was no strong evidence of them as yet. However, they were in place and were quite evident when Mrs. Ferris knew him. The basic governing traits of Ted's personality were likely a part of his personality by the time he graduated from high school.

I concluded the following about his teenage years:

- He hadn't overcome his shyness. He wanted a girlfriend but he was afraid of asking a girl to go out with him. His sex drive was likely strong but he could only satisfy those urges through fantasy

and pornography, and perhaps through voyeurism.
- He put all of his marbles into one basket. He was unable to satisfy his need for a girlfriend when he was in high school so he fantasized about a time in the future where he would have a beautiful coed who would love him as much as he loved her.
- He had a taste of being accepted when he was with his friends skiing. He was accepted by them when he helped campaign for them in high school. This also gave him a little experience in politics.
- Being humiliated by learning he was illegitimate was a major trauma. It added to his identity problems.
- If he was involved in the disappearance of Ann Marie Burr it would have created a major change in him. At first, he would be fearful of getting caught. And if he didn't get caught, he would have to find a way to live with the guilt.
- He wasn't outwardly showing strong characteristics of psychopathy. However, it would be only a few years later that Mrs. Ferris would detect strong moral flaws in him. Assuming the psychopathic behaviors she saw in him didn't suddenly become part of his character it has to be concluded that they started, or were magnified, through his teenage years.

Ted's College Years

Ted didn't find what he was looking for during his freshman year at the University of Puget Sound but he did when he transferred to the University of Washington. He found Marjorie. They hit it off quite well because Ted, through his intelligence and verbal abilities, was able to convince her that he could offer her a secure future consisting of a great career and a family. She was strongly in love with Ted in the beginning and he was madly in love with her. However, his inadequacies and his lying began to show through his fake persona and she became disillusioned.

With Ted, Marjorie was not just a girl he could love, she was his first and only love. She was his sun, stars, and moon combined. She was his entire universe. Marjorie began to see that Ted was more fantasy than reality and she ended the relationship.

Mrs. Ferris knew Ted during this period of his life and she described some very disturbing behaviors including him not keeping jobs; stealing, which included taking waiter's clothing and dressing up in them; borrowing her car to go on "trips;" and being secretive about what he was doing.

When Marjorie ended the relationship, Ted totally fell apart. This was a serious life-changing event for him. He dropped out of college without taking his final exams at Stanford University. Memories at the University of Washington were too painful so even though he tried to take classes there he couldn't finish them.

He went to Philadelphia to visit his grandparents and made a side trip to Vermont where he confirmed he was illegitimate. He returned to Washington, got involved in a political campaign—which worked for him—but his candidate lost so Ted returned to Philadelphia again, this time to go to Temple University. He said he thought he could get a law degree there without having to graduate with a bachelor's degree first. This didn't make sense to me because he was intelligent enough to have checked on that before making the commitment to go back there. It appeared that he was still attempting to adapt to the loss of Marjorie.

I concluded the following about Ted's early adult/college life:

- Ted was able to weather his first romantic encounter with the Asian girl. That was almost a practice run for the next romance and it gave him confidence that it was possible for him to find a girlfriend. However, he was still seeking the one person who could satisfy his dreams.
- Ted's dream failed miserably and he didn't have a plan B. He tried to escape which likely was more than simply traveling back east to visit his grandparents. His hero fantasies likely had changed to hero-sex fantasies and then to sex-control fantasies and possibly to revenge fantasies.
- He was possibly both suicidal and homicidal during this phase of his life.
- There was one positive experience which had an impact on Ted's life. He got involved with the Art Fletcher campaign and was Fletcher's personal driver. However, Fletcher lost so Bundy was again without a purpose.
- Ted was struggling to find an identity. He went to Temple University but that didn't work out. He wasn't fitting in anywhere. He was a ship out in the ocean without a rudder attempting to find an island upon which he could build a career.
- He was almost 23 years old and had dropped out of college three times (Stanford University,

University of Washington, and Temple University). He didn't have a job and didn't have a relationship. He didn't have friends and he had minimal contact with his family. In essence, he had lost everything meaningful to him.

The Liz Kendall period

When he returned from Temple University, he met Liz Kendall and everything temporarily improved. Still, there were additional red flags which suggested Ted was not settling in to a lifestyle which could provide what he needed to begin to mature in a healthy manner. While he often stayed overnight in her apartment, he wasn't willing to move out of his. He had a number of jobs but didn't stay with them for very long. She financially supported him so he was able to finish college at the University of Washington. Throughout the time he was with Liz from 1969 until the summer of 1972 when he graduated, he kept promising her that they would get married as soon as he had a job and could support her. It never happened.

I concluded the following about him during this period of his life:

- He was still struggling for an identity. He was not demonstrating any stability.
- The relationship between Ted and Liz was fraught with problems. He was never satisfied enough to marry her, or even to live with her. However, he couldn't live without her.

- He agreed he would marry her and they got a marriage license. Ted found a pretext to tear up the license so he wouldn't have to keep his commitment. It was also an attempt to get her to stop talking about marriage.
- Liz went out with a couple of guys to make Ted jealous but it backfired. Ted said "that was the last straw!" He appeared to dissociate into a memory—or possibly a flashback—when he told me this.
- Ted was not recovering from his breakup with Marjorie.

June 1972 to January 1974

With support from Liz, Ted graduated from college with a BS degree in psychology in 1972. He began working as a mental health counselor and started dating one or more girls while still telling Liz he planned on marrying her. The girls he went out with described him as having two sides to his personality and behavior. One side was the persona he wanted people to see. Some saw in him as confident and in control, but others felt he was an intellectual phony. He demonstrated sexually aggressive behavior which was frightening to the girls he was with. At times he dissociated into a sexual fantasy when making love. He attempted to reestablish a relationship with Marjorie but it ended in disaster. She interpreted his commitment to marry her as an act of revenge.

I concluded the following about this period of his life:

- His control over his emotions and behavior had seriously deteriorated since he'd graduated from high school in 1965.
- Putting his arm over a sexual partner's throat and choking her during sex bordered on homicide.
- I believe his attempt to reinstate his relationship with Marjorie was an act of desperation rather than an act of revenge. Ted realized that he was almost totally out of control and the Marjorie incident at Christmastime was a last-ditch attempt to keep from killing girls.
- His psychopathic processes were very strong now. Women were to be used. Ted would steal from stores and he was dishonest with others and with himself.

January 1974 to his arrest

When Ted and Marjorie separated on the morning of January 1, 1974, Ted realized that a marriage to her was not the answer. He was totally out of control. In the fall of 1973, he was able to attend law classes at the University of Puget Sound but in the spring of 1974, he couldn't focus on his studies. Once again, he dropped out of school without completing his classes. During the summer of 1974 he went on a rafting trip with Becky, and Larry Voschal and Larry's date. His personality changed so drastically that Larry believed Ted had a multiple personality disorder.

Ted came to Salt Lake City to go to the University of Utah Law School but he only went to a few classes and then stopped. He didn't officially drop out of school and he was able to make up the work he had missed so he was allowed to stay in the program. Liz was still supporting him but she remained in Seattle.

Ted went on dates with some girls and, even though he said they were only friends, they were sexually involved. He said he and Liz were engaged to be married in December, 1975 but it was likely a ruse. Ted became interested in the Church of Jesus Christ of Latter-day Saints and went to their meetings. He lost interest in the Church for a while but then got active again. He was baptized into the LDS Church in early August, 1975. He was arrested on August 16, 1975.

Conclusions regarding this period of his life

- Ted was likely obsessed with killing.
- An attempted homicide occurred a few days after Marjorie returned to her home in California. I had no proof that Ted was the one who did it but it seemed logical that if his attempt to reunite with Marjorie was to avoid killing, it didn't work. Homicides began to occur regularly beginning in February and continued through the summer of 1974. They stopped in that area when Ted went to Salt Lake, at which time homicides in Utah and the adjoining areas began to occur.
- I had enough data to conclude that Ted had a violent personality.

Still, there was strong testimony by people who had worked with Ted. A colleague of Ted's said,

It is clear that other students use him as a standard to emulate.... His personal characteristics are all of the highest standards. Ted is a mature young man who is very responsible and emotionally stable (but not emotionally flat as many students appear—he does get excited or upset appropriately in various situations). He has an excellent sense of humor and in general is a great individual to know as a personal acquaintance. He seems to have many friends and, from my knowledge, he can take charge of a project in an unassuming fashion as well as work smoothly under the direction of others. I am at a loss to delineate any real weaknesses he has.

But then Dr. Evan Lewis indicated in his psychological report:

Mr. Bundy is able to compartmentalize his emotions and thought processes to an unusual degree, possibly to the point that he can dissociate himself from one set of standards so that he can almost totally adapt another. Thus, he is probably capable of giving people very different impressions of himself, depending on what set of standards he chooses to guide his behavior.

Possibly one of the best descriptions of his behavior came from Larry Voschal about the raft trip in the summer of 1974:

His personality went from a very pleasant person to

someone who was practically unbearable to be with. I don't know whether he was tired of his amateur partners or what but it was one of the most unusual personality transformations I've seen. I've been a reporter for about ten years and it's one of the strangest things I've seen. I believe he's got a split personality, a dual personality.

The psychological test data was too clean and of a nature that I often see in people who don't want to reveal themselves. There were a couple of times I saw the angry side of Ted so I knew it was there.

Putting all the information I had gleaned from the test data as well as the phone conversations and the personal interviews with Ted, I arrived at the following conclusions about Ted Bundy, which I put in my report to the court.

1. He is a private person and won't reveal himself to others. He doesn't want to be known by others.
2. He became defensive and evasive when any of his girlfriends tried to get information from him.
3. Outwardly he looks very adequate. This masks strong feelings of inadequacy.
4. He couldn't handle ambiguity (for example, he was obsessively organized and continuously called his investigators for updates so that he would know what the police thought of him).
5. Loss of a father was very significant.
6. He viewed women as more competent than men.

7. He demonstrated a strong dependency on women for emotional support and yet he couldn't settle down with one. He said he resented dependency and yet he seemed to most resent his own dependency.
8. He would get very upset when people would say negative things about him.
9. There were a number of people coming in and out of his life. Most relationships were brief, suggesting instability. He would hurt deeply when he would lose someone. There was a strong sense of futility about him.
10. He is reluctant to accept help or support from anyone (except for financial support). He wants relationships with people on his terms and he wants to be in control of the relationship at all times. He is egocentric. It is extremely important for him to be in control of his emotions, interpersonal relationships and interviews. He has a very strong fear of being hurt and he puts up strong defenses against getting close, including being touched. He has an obsession regarding controlling and structuring and he runs from the situation or relationship when it doesn't work.
11. He shows strong suspiciousness regarding people playing games or trying to trick him and he is always on guard. He is a very perceptive person.
12. There is a strong theme of having been put down, humiliated and made fun of.
13. There is a strong sense of loneliness.
14. He shows a rapid change in moods from pleasant to angry to depressed.

15. He lacks outward indications of guilt and tries to conceal his anxiety. However, he shows it through deep sighs and heavy perspiring.
16. He claims his behavior is not modifiable by fear. "I don't have fears. Fear, pain and punishment don't stick with me." However, this is not true.

I concluded that it was my opinion that Ted's personality fit the crime for which he was found guilty. I submitted my report to the court. Then all hell broke loose.

TWENTY-FIVE

Compartmentalization

There is one additional issue that needs to be addressed. It has often been said that Ted Bundy was a psychopath. It's believed by many that he simply had a desire to go out and kill victims so he did. The belief of this camp is that Ted could turn it on and off at will, and if he wanted to stop, he could. I have no doubt he was showing signs of a psychopathic process at least by the time he was first dating Marjorie. However, I believe that, over time, his desire to hurt girls became an urge that he was often unable to control.

It is reasonable to presume that if a police officer was standing by Carol DaRonch when Ted approached her, he would turn and walk off and not come back. However, the urge at that point of the killing cycle would be very strong and he would have to seek out another victim. When Carol DaRonch was able to get away from him, he *had* to seek out another victim so he went after Debbie Kent a few hours later.

I've had other killers tell me that this is the way it is with them too. If so, it would suggest that the desire to take the life of multiple victims—not mass homicides, but individual events—is something that likely has a subtle beginning, but if the desire is fed it grows and can become so powerful that it has the appearance of a split personality. A possible explanation of how this can occur is through a process that all of us are familiar with: compartmentalization.

Compartmentalization is a process that all of us engage in to one degree or another. It's a complex state of mind on a continuum that can vary from a healthy level, such as with an actor who rehearses a script. He engages in studying the script so intently that when he is portraying that role on stage or in a film, he has a deep sense of being that person. At the other end of the continuum, as it was used by Ted Bundy, compartmentalization can become a very destructive process that can result in violence. This type of compartmentalization is a combination of addiction, intent, imagery, strong unmet needs, and dissociation.

The actor is satisfying his needs through compartmentalization because he creates within his mind the world of his character and he can move around within the sphere of the character he is playing without losing the essence of the part. His role is open for everyone to see. He has an audience who affirms his success in this role. Once he has completed the film or stage production, he can move on to another role. He limits his acting to the medium of the production—the movie set or on stage. Once he leaves that medium within which his craft is performed, he exits the compartment he has created in his mind for that role. If he's playing Hamlet in the theater, for example, he doesn't continue to be Hamlet when he goes to the beach for the weekend with his friends. (There are, of course, examples of actors who stay in character continuously during the production of their play or show, but that does not obviate my point. They are simply remaining in the compartment until that time it suits them to leave.)

The actor's intent is to be able to access the voice, mannerisms, behavior, and emotions of his role on cue as needed. He then has the ability to step out of the role when it's not needed. He creates the compartmentalized role and he controls it. Although it may be somewhat difficult to give up a character once it has become such a powerful part in his life, he has the control over both the creation and the completion. He uses it rather than it using him.

In the case of a Ted Bundy, through fantasy he created a world in which he was able to gratify his sexual needs. The part he played in the fantasy was kept a secret from others. There was no audience to affirm his success and, except for brief sexual satisfaction, there was no success. There was no applause, no congratulations on a job well done. There was no critique of his style and performance. He was the creator of his work and he had no one to tell him it was wrong.

The medium of the production was in his mind as well as in the world around him. He never completely stepped out of his role whether he was living the production in his mind during a crime or was reliving it when he was on the beach. The stage, the props, and the background scenery were only in his mind. The actor steps onto the stage to play out his role. The killer steps from one compartment in his mind into the other. The actor leaves the theater for a day on the beach. The killer shifts from the pathological compartment in his mind back into the socially acceptable compartment of daily living but never completely leaves the theater in his mind and, in fact, it is even more active when he goes to the beach or into a store. It is with him wherever he goes, 24 hours a day, day in and day out.

The intent of the actor is to please his audience, his director, and those who are in the production with him. The intent of the killer is to please himself through his interaction with, generally, one person—the victim. When the actor finishes his part, he receives his accolades and moves on to the next production. The killer never receives the accolades in reality, so he has to pretend that he does, which generally consists of him congratulating himself. He may also attempt to get the victim to express admiration of him.

When a killer finishes a fantasy episode, he feels gratified but not satisfied. There has been a temporary reduction of a powerful drive but an increase in a psychic need. The intensity of the sexual release is so powerful that the killer craves more. As his mind adapts to the experience, the satisfaction diminishes so he has to find ways to keep the experience exciting. In the process of doing this, he progresses from hero fantasies through sexual-control fantasies and possibly to revenge fantasies.

He knows that this style of fantasy life is unacceptable to his friends and family so he continues to keep it secret, and since nobody can criticize him for it, he can do anything during a fantasy episode to satisfy his lusts.

Since at first, he can't experience in reality what he enjoys in fantasy, he enhances his fantasy in an attempt to approximate reality as closely as possible, and thus help him experience it more fully. He blocks out everything going on around him, a process called dissociation. The more he is lonely and uninvolved with satisfying life activities such as relationships, sports, academics, etc., the more he has to turn to fantasy as a vicarious substitution, which he often attempts to do through pornography. The better he becomes at dissociating the world around him during a fantasy, the more real the fantasy feels to him. Instead of fulfilling his need, his need for similar gratification in the real-world increases, which again leads to frustration. He increases the frequency of his sexual fantasy in an attempt to increase the intensity of the experiences, but it still doesn't give him what he is after.

He is soon spending lengthy spans of time in his make-believe world. Since he isn't satisfied with who he is in reality, he creates a more dynamic character in his mind to give the imagery more power. He becomes confused about his identity; he isn't sure which of the two life compartments in his mind is the real one. His growth in his day-to-day life becomes stilted—empty and unfulfilling. He attempts to compensate for this by enhancing his fantasy world and stretching it into his real world. He may molest a woman in fantasy and when he sees a desirable woman later that day, he may relive the same fantasy by imagining he is doing it to her. This increases the reality of the fantasy. Gradually, the fantasy world and the real world begin to meld together. The boundary between the two worlds becomes thinner and more difficult to control.

This becomes a problem because he has to hide his fantasy world from others so they won't become aware of his pathology. He attempts to tighten his real-world compartment and may become obsessive and compulsive in some of his mannerisms. He has to be very careful to keep the two worlds, or two compartments in his mind, separate.

Since it's very difficult—some would say, almost impossible—to have good and evil co-exist within the same mind, he has to find a way to minimize the polarity between the two parts. His criteria for determining right from wrong gradually changes over time. What was wrong for him as a child may become acceptable as an early teen and then desirable when he is in his late teens. He does this by finding justifications for his fantasy life. He may, for example, attempt to convince himself that there is nothing wrong with his daydreams since he isn't actually harming another person.

All this activity increases in intensity and frequency and

the person may become a highly energized assailant in search of a trigger to release the explosion that has been growing within him. Then comes the first victim, and once the offender has stepped over that final boundary—a boundary which has been protecting his shaky identity—his belief about who he is permanently changes, at which time both compartments in his mind will go through an alteration. He soon finds that he is incapable of fighting off the urges to repeat his crime. Now, he *is* the pathology. The day-by-day socially acceptable compartment becomes subservient to the greatly strengthened pathological compartment. Some say that when the killing cycle is triggered into action, they are unable to stop it without something stronger occurring, such as a police officer walking by.

There is an almost total loss of control over his pathology and the person escalates, deteriorates, and then collapses.

TWENTY-SIX

Aftermath

Ted was sentenced to a 5 to Life prison sentence in the Utah State Prison on June 30, 1976. I and other members of the committee were in the courtroom that morning in case we were called upon to answer questions posed by the judge or by Ted or his attorney. I, along with one or two others who were on the committee, sat in the jury seats. In the room were Ted's parents, his girlfriend, the police, some friends, and the press. The room was packed. Ted was sitting with his lawyer, John Connell. Judge Stewart Hansen said he wouldn't allow Ted or his lawyer to cross examine any of us who were on the committee but he would allow Ted to make a statement before he pronounced Ted's sentence.

Ted stood and began speaking. He had some papers in his hand which he began to wave in the air. He was holding my report! With an angry voice and tears in his eyes he said the report was written to fit the crime and was totally inaccurate. Ted sounded sincere and believable. I watched Ted but I could almost feel the eyes of the people in the courtroom looking back and forth between Ted and me. More than one person had tears in their eyes as Judge Hansen told Ted that he would be going to prison for at least five years but he could be kept there for several more. This would be extremely difficult to hear if you were a family member or if Ted were actually innocent, but I felt confident that what I had written was accurate.

Ted was initially placed in the Medium Facility but when he was caught attempting to make a false identification he was transferred to the Maximum Facility. While there, he contacted me and we began having some discussions. After seeing how much hate he expressed towards me in the courtroom, I was very surprised that he was so friendly towards me now.

Towards the end of January, 1977, Ted was taken to Colorado. I wrote the following note:

> January 28, 1977.
> Ted went to court this morning and was told that he would be leaving today or possibly tomorrow to go to Colorado where he will stand trial for murder. In my conversation with him, I found him appearing happy, enthusiastic, and ready for the move. This is typical of him in that when the situation becomes more tense, he shows more enthusiasm. This was especially noted during the assessment procedure when he was on the 90-day program. He has been sticking to a schedule that allows his days to seem short. He gets up in the morning, has a short prayer, and then exercises. After breakfast, he'll take a nap and then about 9:00 a.m. he will begin his work which consists of reading and going over his legal matters. He will also spend some time in the weight room for exercising.

After supper, he writes letters. He is writing to around forty different people and [he] writes as much as sixteen pages. He said he recently wrote two 16-page letters to Liz telling her of things she should do such as finding a mate, etc.

He talked about some of his favorite books. When I asked him to give me the names of five of his best he gave:

- *The Greatest Salesman in the World* by Og Mandino
- *The Hobbit* by J. R. R. Tolkien
- *The Fixer* by Bernard Malamud, which he said was a story about a Jew who received a bum beef and then was finally acquitted.
- *Bury my Heart at Wounded Knee* by Dee Brown
- *Travels with My Aunt* by Graham Green
- *Aldous Huxley: A Biography* by Sybille Bedford
- *For the Defense* by F. Lee Bailey, which is the story about Dr. Shepherd who was arrested, imprisoned, and finally acquitted. Shepherd eventually committed suicide. Ted didn't like this book.

When I asked him if he was anxious about going to Colorado, Ted said, "I have a job to do." He feels that there is no point in feeling anxiety or hate. It's the future that is important.

As is typical of Ted he spends considerable time preparing himself for anything that might happen. He keeps himself psyched up so he can accept anything. When he was put in isolation, he said it was a big turning point in his life because he knew it was the lowest he could go and so he was determined to make his isolation time "good time." He said he succeeded in doing this and he has felt considerable strength because of it.

Ted said that there was one time in his life when he felt he was going to fall apart. This was in December when Liz cut down on her writing for a while. He said he went through a lot of anxiety. This was after I had evaluated him, and although I could see some of the anxiety he was going through, he still had it controlled to the extent that I would not have classified him as "falling apart."

There were a couple of times during this interview that Ted showed some emotion. One time was when he talked about Liz and their breaking up, and another time he showed quite a bit of anger was when he talked about his determination not to be beat by the system (although he did not use those exact words).

I feel that he compartmentalizes very well. I told him that eventually there might be a meshing between all of the anxiety underneath and the enthusiasm, and that the enthusiasm would disintegrate to some degree. He seemed to show some concern and some emotion over this and he indicated to me that he was not suppressing the emotion. He did then say that it is natural to have some anxiety and to suppress it, but he did not feel that it was a big problem for him and that he will succeed in the end.

Overall, Ted seemed to have anxiety that he did not want to show and thus demonstrated an enthusiastic and happy personality instead of the anxiety.

TWENTY-SEVEN

Epilogue

Now at the closing of the day, 40 years after I did this assessment, when we turn out the lights on our discussion and analysis of Theodore Bundy, what conclusions have we come to? Who really was Ted Bundy?

To Louise Cowell Bundy, Ted was an unfortunate mistake. However, she accepted him and she and John Bundy brought up Ted and his four younger siblings in a religious home. There were no indications of physical or sexual abuse. The perception people had of him then was that he was a nice boy who was intelligent but somewhat shy. He was obedient and not rebellious. He indicated to me he didn't have a lot of supervision so he was free to make his own decisions as long as it didn't openly violate his parents' rules.

But everything wasn't going well during his early childhood. When he was only four years old, he was taken from the home of his grandparents and his two loving teenage aunts and found himself among strangers in an unfamiliar environment. His mother soon married John Bundy and his half-siblings came soon after. His mother's time was taken up with her new family. Ted said his relationship with his stepfather was largely a one-way affair with his stepfather often correcting him for things he believed Ted was doing wrong.

Ted also had minimal communication with his mother, which was actually quite common in those days. Much later, his mother told me that Ted was always a good boy who was successful in everything he did, but according to Ted this wasn't true. Ted struggled to be successful but he never reached the level of achievement that he hoped for. The fact that he felt humiliated when he wasn't in the top reading circle in 4th grade emphasized the problem. His mother told me he was good in sports, but this was also not true according to Ted.

Ted was a lonely boy. He didn't feel he fit in with his family, but this went unrecognized because Ted was a "good boy" and didn't make waves.

There was one thing that was quite good in Ted's life when he was young. He had friends in the neighborhood and they would play games and sit on someone's porch in the evening and talk. Ted was part of this circle and the other kids accepted him and were friendly towards him. Ted may have fit in better with them than with his family. Later, when he was an adult and girlfriends wanted to know about his family, or when they wanted Ted to take them to visit his family, he wouldn't do it. The impression some obtained from him was that he was ashamed of his family and he only went back to visit them because he wanted to be with his younger brother, Richard.

Ted was not mean when he was a child. He cared for people, which was confirmed by many who knew him.

There was a Mrs. Louise S who sent a letter to the court. She wrote,

I feel I must write to you in behalf of Theodore R. Bundy. Until Ted graduated from Wilson High School, he lived one block from us. As a classmate and a friend of our son, he spent many hours at our house and beach place. After Ted left Tacoma, he would come to see Mr. S and me two or three times a year. We looked forward to his visits and enjoyed them very much. We were happy to have him spend any of his free time at our beach cabin. If, however, we ran into Ted at the University of Washington District, he was always open, smiling and glad to see us. We are proud of the way he applied himself to his chosen career and we even looked forward to voting for him some day.

In 1970, our three-and-a-half-year-old granddaughter strayed from her parents at Green Lake in Seattle. I only wish I could impress you with a double surprise when a young man pulled a child from the water and it was their daughter! And her savior, good old Ted Bundy!

I know the Ted Bundy we know and admire is innocent. I realize Ted's career has been destroyed and the bizarre perversity has made and will continue to make his life difficult.

Please do not allow Ted to be unjustly sentenced to unfair confinement as well.

There's no doubt that Ted was liked and respected by many people. However, all wasn't as peaceful and secure as he wanted people to believe. He found a release from loneliness through fantasy and, when he reached puberty, got involved with pornography and crime stories. Up to that time of his life Ted was not significantly different than most boys his age. He was lonely but it wasn't his loneliness that turned him into a serial killer. It was that his loneliness and daydreaming went a different direction when he got into pornography.

It should be noted that the pornography of Ted's early years was not equivalent to what is considered pornography in the 21st century. Pornography at the time included any content which held "no socially redeeming value." This included, among other things, violent and erotic fiction, photos and graphic descriptions of murders and other death-related subjects such as crime-scene photos and autopsies, as well as the erotic or graphically sexual photos and films that we think of as pornography today. The society of Ted's time shunned this kind of content as well as those who consumed it, and for a young man like Ted to access it would be exceedingly risky to his reputation, and consequently all the more tantalizing to someone with an active fantasy life who had few other outlets for risk taking and excitement. This, combined with the strong emotional and physical release of masturbation, may have led Ted to seek out these "deviant" materials for the thrill of it, at least at the beginning. Later, as Ted's rape fantasies flourished, he would have become both comfortable with the thought of violent rape in a fantasy context as well as intrigued by what the actual experience of violent rape and murder might entail.

The practice of reading and consuming pornographic material continued and increased throughout Ted's teenage years. Dr. Art Norman, a psychologist, interviewed Ted in Florida. Regarding the issue of crime stories and hard-core porn, Ted said the following about the type of material he looked for to whet and satisfy his burgeoning appetite:

> I always sought out stories where the guy confessed. I wanted first-hand stuff. I didn't want the police version.... The best articles always had crime scene photos. That's what I went for. I became something of a connoisseur.... If I had, under different circumstances, been able to channel all that creativity, all that time—masses of time—into law or into anything else, with my intelligence it could have been astounding. And yet, it went in a different direction. And so, I became something of a connoisseur of these kinds of photos and I knew where to get pictures of crime scene photographs. I also became very adept at going into medical school libraries and getting their autopsy texts, especially photographs of autopsies and crime scenes involving young women who had been murdered. This was the sort of thing I got into. That was an interest that was part of the phase of my life before I ever harmed anyone.

Ted showed no strong anger as a child or as a teenager. Marjorie didn't see anger in Ted when she was dating him. Criminal tendencies were detected by Mrs. Ferris but his anger wasn't apparent until Marjorie broke up with him. Both times Ted went back to Philadelphia he got more heavily involved with pornographic fantasy. There is reason to believe that he killed his first two victims on his second trip back there, which would have caused a dramatic change in his identity at that time.

Elizabeth "Liz" Kendall was a breath of fresh air for him and she provided stability. She put him through college and supported him financially when he was unable to keep a job. She was always by his side when he needed emotional support.

However, Ted was a victim of the night and he couldn't give up his obsessive voyeuristic habits. His dark side was extremely strong at this point, and his attempt to dissociate into dramatic passionate fantasies resulted in his giving over his power to his developing dark side. By the time he graduated from college in 1972 and dated two girls in Seattle, his anger and sexual aggression were out of control.

In the summer of 1973, he attempted to bring Marjorie back into his life. The possibility of a relationship began during the summer and appeared to be strong when they got together in the fall. By Christmas, she was ready to marry him but he realized that he couldn't marry her. While one reason was because she got too upset with him, the primary reason was because he couldn't give up his night prowling and his sexual fantasies while watching women undress. The dark side of him was too powerful to give up and he couldn't do his night prowling while living with a woman.

When Marjorie flew back to San Francisco with a promise of marriage, Ted gave up any attempt to control his sexual aggression.

Throughout the spring of 1974, Ted compulsively murdered one woman after another. His approach to his victims reflected a skilled homicidal technique with great confidence. In the summer of 1974, his friends on the raft trip witnessed such a dramatic change in his personality while going down a river that he was described as having a split personality.

Ted went to Salt Lake to continue with his education (or possibly to get out of the area where he was suspected of some of the murders) but he couldn't stop killing. Finally, he was caught, tried, found guilty, and sentenced to prison.

When he was transferred to Colorado he escaped. After he was caught, he called me to see what I thought about his escape. He said he was planning to leave the country because even if he was eventually found innocent of the DaRonch crime his reputation would prevent him from ever practicing law. However, when he did escape a second time, instead of leaving the country, he went to the northeast and then to Florida. Again, he couldn't stop killing. He was apprehended, tried for murder, and executed.

Final Comment

Ted Bundy is gone. Executed. He was willing to give the names of many of his victims, and at least we can thank him for that. Ted attempted to make the point several times that he was no different than anyone else and that anybody could become a Ted Bundy. Did he really believe that or was it simply a justification to ease his guilt?

Currently, it's not serial killers that are in the headlines but mass killers and terrorists. It's difficult to understand why a person would want to hunt down and kill victims one at a time, but it's more difficult to fathom why a young man would go into a school loaded with weapons for the sole purpose of killing classmates.

Either there is something that we are not understanding regarding the development of the violent mind or possibly we already have enough information to do something about it, but we are just not doing it yet.

Appendix I

A CONVERSATION WITH TED

On October 3, 1977, a colleague of mine, Dr. Allan Roe, and I went into Salt Lake City for lunch. When we got back to the prison there was a message waiting for me to call an operator in Salt Lake. I called her back and she said Ted Bundy had called from Colorado and he wanted me to return his call. He had escaped from jail and had been caught. Now he was back in jail and he was calling *me*?

I was intrigued as to why this serial killer would want to talk to me. During the call, I learned that he had called twice previously but had been unable to get in touch with me. He wanted to make sure we connected this time. I had not talked with Ted since my session with him just before he went to Colorado. What was so important to make three attempts to get hold of me?

I called the operator in Salt Lake who connected me with the jail in Colorado and then the connection went to Ted's cell. He had his own credit card to pay for the call.

Ted asked how I was doing. I answered,
I'm doing all right, Ted. How are you doing?

Well, I'm hanging in there. I just got the bug last week and just wanted to chat with you briefly because obviously I've been away for a long time.

How are things going for you over there?
Well, quite well, frankly, I was just talking to someone the other day and the experience of coming over here is one of those, you know, good things, bad things experiences. If I hadn't come over here, I probably wouldn't be looking at a new trial in the Carol DaRonch case and a number of things have opened up and I suppose that if I had to spend several years behind bars, I might as well spend a little here, a little there. (laughs)

Ted was in Colorado because he was being investigated for a homicide, which was bad for him. On the other hand, he was saying that had he not come to Colorado he wouldn't have obtained information that might allow him to have a new trial on the DaRonch case, which was good as he saw it. As with previous conversations I had had with him he was attempting to tell me he wasn't guilty of that crime. He sounded optimistic. Why was it so important for him to bring up the DaRonch case?

Are they treating you pretty good?
Well, yeah, sure they are. They've developed this paranoia about me. They have this unrealistic fear that I'm going to escape or something.

In essence, he was saying: It's silly that they would believe that I might be thinking about escaping again. These guys are paranoid. They are overreacting.

I can't imagine where they're getting that from. (both laugh)

Yeah, exactly (laughs). Al, I just wanted to call you up, mainly…there are a lot of things that've been happening. My escape venture, which has caused a great furor of activity around here and I guess some complicity over there, and now we're looking at what looks like a 95% chance of a new trial in the Carol DaRonch case. And this case over here gets curiouser and curiouser because they've added a couple of additional Utah transactions, alleged transactions, in an attempt to gain a conviction in the Colorado case.

I don't know… I've been so overwhelmed by work recently, that uh… You know, there's just a lot to do. You know, way back when, I guess it was back in April, when I decided to represent myself in this case, I could just… (laughs) I was thinking to myself, I could hear Al Carlisle saying, "Yeah, I knew you'd try something like that." (laughs)

Yeah, I assumed you would. (laughs)

Why did he bring this up? He almost told me why he called, but before he could say just what it was, he mentioned the Carol DaRonch case again and reiterated that it was almost certain that he would get a new trial. Was he really trying to convince me he was innocent? If so, why was this so important? He had been telling everyone that he had never hurt anyone, and many people seemed convinced that he could not have committed the DaRonch crime. I, on the other hand, had submitted a report to the court saying I thought he was violent. Was he trying to say I was wrong? Perhaps.

I remember one time you commented… I can't remember if it was something… I think it was something I read in one your reports, quite frankly. Ah, how did you say it? That I can't delegate responsibility or something to that effect, I don't know. I don't think that's exactly the way you put it, but something more or less that I like to do things myself and I have a hard time entrusting things to others.

Uh huh.

I was wondering, I know you are really at arm's length on this thing and we haven't really talked personally obviously since the latter part of January. But I've been wondering if you've had any impression about all that you've been hearing about me and ah… and ah…

How do you mean?

Well, like the escape and everything. I wonder what your impression of that was, again just from a party who knows me but didn't have an opportunity to speak to me after that happened.

The call reminded me of a boy who called his father wanting to know what he thought of the ball game on TV the night before. Did he want my approval, or forgiveness? Did he want to know if I was angry at him? I was puzzled about what he wanted from me. I decided that rather than answering the question I would take this opportunity to learn more about why he escaped. He was caught attempting to make a false ID when he was in prison so it wasn't surprising that he jumped at the opportunity to escape from jail in Colorado.

I had mixed impressions. I was wondering if you were really getting uptight and the pressure looked like it was on. I was wondering if it was getting to look like, in your mind, you were going to be convicted, so when the opportunity was there you just took it. In your own mind, what was happening?

You know, I'd given it a great deal of thought. I'd been moved from Aspen… I'd been in the Pitkin County Jail, which is in Aspen, from January 31st until April the 11th, which is 73 days. I have all this memorized. In Aspen, it was an open affair. It's seven cells and all the doors are open all the time. The place had been built in 1887. Here was where I could come out and relate and talk to other prisoners going in their cell. Something like the State Prison [in Utah], not like Max [Maximum Security Facility in Utah]. And then they moved me down here—this is part of the escape because I was a security risk. They put me in a six by twelve by eight-foot-high cell and ordered no one to speak to me. Quite frankly, that's why I decided to represent myself. Concrete, solid steel doors with [a] small window. This is worse than the hole. Honest Al, this was worse than the hole in Max, because there you could at least talk to people and see people. This [tension] was building up and building up and building up, and over the months I'd noticed a number of opportunities to just walk right out, walk right out of the court house, but I didn't know how to put it all together. I was very concerned about what people would think. People say, weren't you afraid that somebody would shoot you or something?

No, it was one of the lower fears in my hierarchy of fears. But I don't know, that day I came there and I thought a great deal about escape and I didn't know if I had the guts to do it, quite frankly. The guard went outside for a smoke and there was not one person in the whole courtroom. You'd have to see the courthouse in Aspen to understand. The windows were open and the fresh air was blowing through and the sky was blue and I said, I'm ready to go, and I walked to the window and I jumped out. (laughs) And I started chugging.

I had no plan. I had nobody helping me. I had no money and no nothing. I just ran right up into the mountains.

But anyway, you know when I was recaptured and they brought me back in, I spoke very freely about my adventures during those six days. It was something I couldn't deny. But one of the investigators working on my case came into the room after I had been there some time and said, Well, would you like to talk about the Campbell case? Would you like to tell me all about it now, Ted? Would you like to confess and all this stuff? I could see the twinkle in his eye. He thought that I had panicked and the gig was up and I was ready to bust open. And I told him, Mike, listen, I just went out the window because I wanted to be free.

It wasn't a fear of conviction because I believed then and I believe more firmly now that I'll be acquitted. And not only that I'll get a new trial on DaRonch. The irony of it all, Al, is that probably the only solid conviction they will have on me will be the escape. Honest to God, I just got sick and tired of being locked up.

I kept saying to myself, Ted, in the event that you're acquitted here in Colorado and you go back to Utah and let's say you got a new trial on DaRonch, which I estimate would take three years, because even if we won at the trial court level with a new trial the state would appeal, and unless the Supreme Court overturns we'll have to go to Federal Court. The Federal Court takes years and years, and even if I got a new trial on DaRonch three years from now there's a chance I could be convicted just basically on just the publicity of the whole thing. I mean I'm pretty notorious. And if I was acquitted three or four years from now on the DaRonch case, what would I have left?

Maybe unrealistically, but I asked myself could you go to law school? Could you go back to Liz? Would your friends be able to look you in the eye? Could you be Ted Bundy again? I figured, whether you're free tomorrow or you're free four years from now you're still going to have to make an entirely new life and really hide from the old life, whether legitimately or illegitimately. So those are the priorities.

Is it possible that he was telling me that he would make another attempt to escape if he got the chance? Ted was a very perceptive person and likely memorized everything he could about the jail he was in, including the routines of the staff. His ploy was to be friends with everyone so they would begin to trust him. Then he would strike. This was the same approach he used with his victims. Ted continued,

I wasn't up against a wall. Maybe it was something I could have done then, something I could wait to do but I was honestly just fed way up above my chin with being locked up. And, it was just one of those things. I still have the scars and blisters on my feet. I'm sitting here barefooted... (laughs) Running around in the mountains.

It was an extraordinary experience because I thought I was... I'm a pretty strong-willed person. But, believe it or not, it was the body that was strong but the mind that was weak. The morning after.... Well, I ran up, you know, like 4,000 feet of very steep hill. Actually, Aspen mountain, and over the other side. They didn't know where in the world I was, and I was feeling really good that evening, and I started hiking up; and if I could have kept hiking I would have been long gone. But a very cold, sleet rainstorm hit me. I got very cold and I went into a state of shock. And I managed to find my way back to the cabin. There was no way to get into it and here I was shivering and hungry and cold and it was raining and blowing. And early the next morning, about 7:00 in the morning, I was just sitting there seriously considering giving myself up. It was just a complete mind blow for me to have longed for freedom for so long and now, like I was living my ultimate dream. All of a sudden, I was willing to throw it away because I was cold and hungry.

I got in the cabin and recuperated, believe it or not, and had a second chance at it. And then I made a wrong turn and then I hurt my knee. Three or four days of high altitude and cold got to me and again my mind got weak. That night I walked back into Aspen. No one knew me. People saw me, no one could recognize me. I was totally disoriented. It's something I've never known before. I just laid down like an animal ready to die. It was just an incredible experience. I was disoriented and quite frankly I foolishly just hopped in a car and drove. I knew I would get caught. I mean, I didn't want to get caught but I knew it would happen. I was just so tired and I said, well, let's see what will happen. It was a fluke, actually. They stopped me. When I got captured, I just stood there. Anyway, that was one of the more profound experiences of being over here. It certainly did cause a furor.

Ted and I talked for a couple more minutes. I asked him about my coming out to Colorado and talking more about this and other aspects of his history. Ted was amenable to this, but before I could get over there, he escaped again.

The impression I got from that call was that Ted was lonely and he had a need to talk. In my work at the prison, I had a number of guys who seemed to have a need to talk, and often it was about their crimes. They seemed to want someone to understand them. If they were only trying to convince me that they were not guilty I wouldn't have continued talking to them. But it was interesting to me that so many hardened criminals would open up and talk about very personal events in their lives, including violent crimes they had committed that they had never been arrested for.

I learned that psychopaths could seem to feel regret for their crimes.

Appendix II

A LETTER FROM TED

I recently received a copy of a letter that Ted wrote to me in 1976 when he was still in the diagnostic program at the prison. The letter – well, actually letters—were evidently in the possession of one of Ted's lawyers before he became his own attorney, and was acquired by a documentary filmmaker who interviewed me and showed me the letters. It is unclear why the letters never surfaced before now. I'm very pleased that I was able to get copies of them.

It appears that Ted started a letter but wasn't satisfied with it so he rewrote it. The letter was addressed to me and it is in Ted's handwriting. It's a fascinating letter but I wonder why Ted wrote it. And why didn't I receive it at that time? As far as I know, he didn't write a similar letter to other members of the evaluation team. Here is his first attempt at the letter, exactly as written.

May 11, 1976
Theodore Bundy (signature)

Dear Dr. Carlisle,

Recently a fellow inmate gave me a tattered, year-old issue of the National Geographic. One article entitled 'Six Months Alone in a Cave' attracted my attention. It was a scientific chronical which sought to describe the effects of confinement and isolation on mental and biological rhythms. The study intrigued me because I am so acutely aware of my own reactions to confinement of a different variety.

Michael Siffre, the subject of the experiment and the author of the article began with these words:

Overcome with lethargy and bitterness I sit on a rock and stare at my campsite in the bowels of midnight Cave, near Del Rio, Texas. Behind me lie a hundred days of solitude; ahead loom two and a half more lonely months. But I—a wildly displaced Frenchman—know none of this, for I am living "beyond time," divorced from calendars and clocks and from sun and moon, to help determine among other things, the natural rhythms of human life.

While I am not, like Mr. Siffre, confined to determine the natural rhythms of human life, I am very conscious of my own particular rhythms, my reactions to incarceration, and feel that I, too, am living "beyond time" divorced from the elements of my existence which have tuned the rhythms of my own life over the years. With the empathy that only experience brings, I read Siffre's entry after 77 day[s] in the Midnight Cave that "I am in excellent form. I notice, though, a fragility of memory. I recall nothing from yesterday. Even events of this morning are lost. If I do not write things down immediately, I forget them."

Incarceration, like confinement in the cave, dulls the memory. Uneventful thoughtless days blend into one another. Living only in the moment, isolated from the schedule which wound my clock on the outside, I see days pass swiftly and unintelligibly by. There is a negative reinforcement in not thinking and remembering because by not doing so I am reminded of the cruel reality of prison. The time passes quickly.

This outcome would be nothing less than justice by default, satisfying some vague notion of punishment possessed by the community and subjecting me to the degrading and deteriorating environment of prison.

The prospects for a resolution of this quandary are not bright. I am sure you appreciate the difficulty encountered by your colleagues, and, perhaps, you might even concur with their predilection not to formulate any prognosis in my case. On the other hand, I would hope that your exposure to prison life about the modifying impact incarceration is reputed to have on a person.

[End of first letter]

May 14, 1976

Theodore Bundy

Dr. Al Carlisle
Diagnostic Unit
Utah State Prison

Dear Dr. Carlisle,
Recently a fellow inmate gave me a tattered year-old issue of the National Geographic. One article entitled 'Six Months Alone in a Cave' attracted my attention. It was a scientific chronical which sought to describe the effects of confinement and isolation on mental and biological rhythms. The study intrigued me because I am so acutely aware of my own reactions to confinement of a different variety.

Michel Siffre, the subject of the experiment and the author of the article began with these words:

Overcome with lethargy and bitterness, I sit on a rock and stare at my campsite in the bowels of midnight Cave, near Del Rio, Texas. Behind me lie a hundred days of solitude; ahead loom two and a half more lonely months. But I — a widely displaced Frenchman — know none of this, for I am living "beyond time", divorced from calendars and clocks, and from sun and moon, to help determine

Bundy Letter One, Page 1

among other things, the natural rhythms of human life...."

While I am not, like Mr. Siffre, confined to determine the natural rhythms of human life, I am very conscious of my own particular rhythms, my reactions to incarceration, and feel that I, too, am living "beyond time", divorced to the elements of my existence which have timed the rhythms of my own life over the years. With the empathy that only experience brings, I read Siffre's entry after 77 days in the midnight cave that "I am in excellent form. I notice, though, a fragility of memory. I recall nothing from yesterday. Even events of this morning are lost. If I do not write things down immediately, I forget them."

Incarceration, like confinement in the cave, dulls the memory. Uneventful, thoughtless days blend into one another. Living only in the moment, isolated from the schedule which wound my clock on the outside, I see days pass swiftly and unintelligibly by. There is a negative reinforcement in not thinking and remembering because by not doing so I am reminded of the cruel reality of prison. So time passes quickly.

Bundy Letter One, Page 2

This outcome would be nothing less than justice by default, satisfying some vague notion of punishment possessed by the community and subjecting me to the degrading and deteriorating environment of prison.

The prospects for a resolution of this quandary are not bright. I am sure you appreciate the difficulty encountered by your colleagues, and, perhaps, you might even concur with their predilection not to formulate any prognosis in my case. On the other hand, I would hope that your exposure to prison life about the modifying impact incarceration is reputed to have on a person.

Bundy Letter One, Page 3

Appendix III

Evidently, when Ted read through what he had written, he felt it wasn't strong enough. It's as if when he wrote the last paragraph, he became aware that he was specifically addressing me. A major difference between the two letters is that in the first attempt Ted is speaking in a general manner, while in the completed letter Ted is speaking directly to me, as if he was sitting across the desk from me pleading with me to see the error of my perception of him. Here's his final letter:

May 11, 1976
Theodore Bundy (signature)

Dr. Al Carlisle
Diagnostic Unit
Utah State Prison

Dear Dr. Carlisle,

Recently, a fellow inmate gave me a tattered year-old

issue of the National Geographic. One article, entitled 'Six Months in a Cave', attracted my attention. It was a scientific chronical which sought to describe the effects of confinement and isolation on mental and biological rhythms. The study intrigued me because I am so acutely aware of my reactions to the isolation and confinement of prison.

Michel Siffre, the subject of the experiment and the author of the article began with these words: "Overcome with lethargy and bitterness, I sit on a rock and stare at my campsite in the bowels of Midnight Cave, War Del Rio, Texas. … I am living "beyond time," divorced from calendars and clocks and from sun and moon, to help determine, among other things, the natural rhythms of human life …"

While I am not, like Mr. Siffre, confined to determine the natural rhythms of human life, I am very conscious of my particular rhythms, my reactions to incarceration. Imprisonment or experimental isolation, an experience common to both of these conditions is a sense of living "beyond time," and [is] a paralysis born by lethargy and bitterness.

Under conditions which induce emotional distress and deteriorated mental functioning, how can a psychologist, such as yourself, begin to distinguish traits distorted or produced by the deprivations of the prison environment from traits (characteristics/behaviors) displayed by an inmate when he is free to respond (in) a community environment? Are you, like Mr. Siffre, simply measuring reactions to stress, isolation, and confinement or can you naturally assess the real person, uncontaminated by imprisonment? I ask these questions because I am concerned that a confounding variable may be interfering with the analysis made of an inmate. Hostility, anger, bitterness, neurosis, defensiveness, or antisocial attitudes may be a response to the pressures and realities of prison and not indices which truly reflect the character of the individual you are examining. Can you make the distinctions?

You have made some thoughtful judgments about me. You have indicated that I am hard to get to know, that I am angry, and that I am precise, objective and somewhat impersonal when discussing myself. These are accurate observations about Theodore Bundy the prisoner, but what about Theodore Bundy the person before he was subjected to months of intense stress and incarceration? Had we the opportunity to meet under different circumstances, socially and informally, what would your impression have been then?

The point I am trying to make involves normality versus abnormality versus adaptation. How would you react, how would any average citizen react, if you were taken from your familiar, everyday life and place[d] in the bizarre atmosphere of prison? Would you be angry, suspicious of authority, protective and defensive? Your adaptation may be reasonable when the circumstances are considered, but abnormal when compared to some abstract, normative scale.

Prison has had its effect on me. Lethargy, bitterness, depression, antisocial attitudes, and disorganized thought processes have *all* been reactions apparent to me. But I resist the destruction of my personality and myself and I will not be lured into the common weaknesses which prison breeds. I become objective about my situation because it raises me above the chaos and corruption of the moment. Defensive?

Perhaps. I like myself, too much, to allow prison to make me a cruel, insensitive, violent and anti-establishment convict just to survive.

Beneath the reactions to confinement there remains the essential ingredients of my personality. I have not concealed them from you. Still you seem uncomfortable. Why? What are you looking for? Is it some intuitive feeling which says you do not know me? Unfortunately, our relationship is artificial and forced by the pressures of time. You cannot know me and I cannot know you in such a short time.

[End of letter]

May 11, 1976

Dr. Al Carlisle
Diagnostic Unit
Utah State Prison

Theodore Bundy

Dear Dr. Carlisle,

Recently, a fellow inmate gave me a tattered, year old issue of the National Geographic. One article entitled "Six Months in a Cave", attracted my attention. It was a scientific chronicle which sought to describe the effects of confinement and isolation on mental and biological rhythms. The study intrigued me because I am so acutely aware of my reactions to the isolation and confinement of prison.

Michel Siffre, the subject of the experiment and the author of the article, began with these words:

"Overcome with lethargy and bitterness, I sit on a rock and stare at my campsite in the bowels of Midnight Cave, near Del Rio, Texas. . . . I am living 'beyond time', divorced from calendars and clocks, and from sun and moon, to help determine, among other things, the natural rhythms of human life..."

Bundy Letter Two, Page 1

(2)

While I am not, like Mr. Siffre, confined to determine the natural rhythms of human life, I am very conscious of my particular rhythms, my reactions to incarceration. Imprisonment or experimental isolation, an experience common to both of these conditions is a sense of living "beyond time", and a paralysis born by lethargy and bitterness.

Under conditions which induce emotional distress and deteriorated mental functioning, how can a psychologist, such as yourself, begin to distinguish traits distorted or produced by the deprivations of the prison environment from traits (characteristics/behaviors) displayed by an inmate when he is free to respond a community environment? Are you, like Mr. Siffre, simply measuring reactions to stress, isolation, and confinement or can you actually assess the real person, uncontaminated by imprisonment.

I ask these questions because I am concerned that confounding variables may be interfering with the analysis made of an inmate. Hostility, anger, bitterness, neurosis, dependence, or anti-social attitudes may be a response to the pressures and realities of prison and not

Bundy Letter Two, Page 3

(4)

Prison has had its effect on me. Lethargy, bitterness, depression, anti-social attitudes, and disorganized thought processes have all been reactions apparent to me. But I resent the destruction of my personality and myself, and I will not be lured into the common weaknesses which prison breeds. I become objective about my situation because it raises me above the chaos and corruption of the moment. Defensive? Perhaps. I like myself, too much, to allow prison to make me a cruel, insensitive, violent and anti-establishment convict just to survive.

Beneath the reactions to confinement there remains the essential ingredients of my personality. I have not concealed them from you. Still you seem uncomfortable. Why? What are you looking for? Do I have some intuitive feeling which says you do not know me? Unfortunately, our relationship is artificial and forced by the pressures of time; you cannot know me and I cannot know you in such a short time.

Bundy Letter Two, Page 4

Appendix IV

INTERVIEW

Dan Clark
March 23, 2017

Dan Clark was a police officer who was put in charge of searching for one of Ted Bundy's victims. The following are excerpts from an interview I had with him:

Dan: When I was working with the BYU [Brigham Young University] Police Department. A little gal came up missing who was there for a youth conference. The LDS Church sponsors these kids to come to BYU and they have a three to four day visit at the university, and they get involved with games and activities to help these kids grow, and then they have a dance, either Friday or Saturday depending on the schedule, but they have a formal dance and one of the little gals came up missing on Friday. She changed clothes and got ready and walked towards the dance on her own and she never arrived. She was wearing a long yellow formal and never showed up. I got the call when I was the investigator on duty, and we started looking for her.

We interviewed the kids that were there with her, her friends and associates from the group that had walked some distance with her, and nobody had any clue on where she had gone. In those first few hours, there was not a lot to go on. We didn't have pictures; we didn't have anything. The parents made contact with us the next day. I am a little ahead of myself… The friends had notified the parents and on Saturday morning, I got the call and we started looking for her.

We made contact with the bus stations and nobody had seen her there. We started looking around the foothills thinking that maybe she just wandered off. The parents indicated that they had some trouble with her earlier on but thought that everything had been resolved, so they didn't think that she just wandered off. We had no idea about Ted Bundy at the time.

Al: What was the date?

Dan: Oh gosh, I can't remember the dates now. I wouldn't even offer to guess. It has been 30 years, but Bundy had yet to be identified for anything. He was currently a student at the University of Utah Law School and this was before he picked up the one gal that escaped from him.

Al: Carol DaRonch.

Dan: Yeah, in Salt Lake. She was working at the Cottonwood Mall. He picked her up and she escaped. She got a really good description of his Volkswagen and maybe a plate number. I think it was Salt Lake PD that picked him up and served a search warrant. They found hair and he was sequentially charged. But that happened after this little gal, I guess we can use her name, Sue Curtis, had disappeared. So somewhere between the time that he was in law school and when he finally got arrested in Salt Lake is when Sue disappeared. I apologize that I don't have the dates. If you need them, I can dig them up.

Al: Was it spring or summer?

Dan: This would have been during the summer. That is when most of these youth conferences are. I think at the time Sue was a high school sophomore or junior from the Bountiful or Woods Cross area. She just vanished. We didn't have a clue what had happened to her. This went on for several years. That first year, the parents went to the University of Utah and listened to a lecture by a psychic. They hired him and also hired a private investigator.

The psychic told them that from what he could see she had been picked up by someone that she thought she knew and she was taken up a canyon with red rocks, past an old railroad trestle, and had been dumped. That was all he had given them. So, the parents called me and gave me that information and we started looking up the various canyons around Provo.

When you go far enough up Spanish Fork Canyon, there are some red rock cliffs up there and an old railroad trestle. So, we started searching. But it had been a couple of years and we thought that because of the deer hunters in the area, that if she had been dumped up in that canyon, she would have been found. The likelihood of her body being discovered the first couple of years is pretty good, so that trail went cold. We had, over the course of the investigation, gotten pictures and distributed them. We got dental records in case we found something, and every time a female body was found, the medical examiner would pull up her dental records and see if it was her. An interesting thing about her, about Sue, when you look at Bundy's victims, their physical description, these girls could be sisters. Of the 30 or so pictures [of women] that they suspect that he was responsible for killing, long straight brown hair, parted in the middle, same facial characteristics, same height, same body build, he had a type that he was attracted to. You have seen the pictures and Sue Curtis's would fit right in the middle of them and there would be no question. During the time that this was going on he was driving his little VW bug and had been around this area. One of his victims was the Kent girl.

Al: Debbie Kent. From Bountiful. He got her out of a high school theater where they were having a play.

Dan: Her body has never been found, has it? Above Manti…no, Fairview…they found part of a body up there, years after, and they had an arm but it disappeared. They had it for years and never had DNA tested. Nobody knew about DNA back then. By the time they thought that he may have been involved with her the evidence had been lost.
So your buddy Wally Barrus and Jim from BYU that flew these model aircraft with cameras in them would

go out and film areas in the morning or late afternoon with the sun coming in at an oblique angle and look for places that had been disturbed, and so Jim went down and flew this area about Fairview where they thought that they had found this body, and there were a couple of sites that they went back in and excavated but they couldn't find anything. So, we thought about using Wally, but by the time we had an idea about Bundy or where we thought this gal might be, this body, or the parts of a body, were found above Fairview, and we didn't know if they were Sue C or Debbie Kent's remains. We just didn't know.

That petered out. Basically, it just dried up. It went totally cold until Bundy got bagged up in Florida for beating that girl with the piece of a tree branch, killing her in her sorority room. Those killings and those victims looked just like Sue. Over the course of these years, when we found out about Bundy, I started looking at the pictures of his victims from up in Washington/Oregon areas, where they figured he killed 20 or 30, and I went to my boss. I had those pictures, and I put Sue Curtis's photo in there. I said, is there any question in your mind where she went? Who got her? And he kind of poopooed the idea, but I figured that Bundy had taken her. But here he is in Florida; he has finally been arrested after he escaped from Colorado.

Al: He was in prison in Utah and we gave him up to Colorado because they were doing an investigation and he escaped.

Dan: Jumped out the courtroom window.

Al: Yes, jumped out the courtroom window, and he got caught and came back and he was there. He called me and we had about a 15-minute telephone conversation.

Dan: You interviewed him at the state prison?

Al: I did the psych evaluation on him. Then he escaped the second time and went up Northeast and then down to Florida.

Dan: When all of these pictures started coming in and we figured out he was in the area, we thought why not? We thought that he would be good for it. I wanted to go to Florida and interview him. I had a boss that was all about pinching pennies and wouldn't let me go. He said, "I bet he is from Salt Lake County. My buddies will do that one." Nobody went down to interview him.

So, the clock is running on his execution, the stays are exhausted and a Salt Lake County Deputy went down and interviewed him at length, at least several hours, to talk about Debbie Kent and these other gals, but I am not sure what they found out. My boss would not let me go down and I will always hold it against him because the family needs some closure. They had her declared legally dead and had a memorial service and everything else.

Over the course of all these years the family moved from Bountiful and they ended up in a little town called Wellington out by Price. Mr. Curtis was running a sporting goods store out there, and they lived on a hill outside of Wellington in a nice neighborhood and it had a view to the south and to the west and even to the east for miles out on the highway. We maintained contact over the years and any time anything would happen I would call them or they would call me. Good people, just solid people. So here comes Bundy's execution and in the elevator going to the execution chamber the assistant warden asked him if there is anybody else. He had already talked to the Salt Lake County detective for a couple of hours, but he didn't care about our case, he cared about his own.

I wanted to go down there, even make a phone call, if I had been allowed to call him on the phone and ask him about our case, because Bundy freely gave it up in the elevator. Bundy said to the assistant warden, "Yes there was a little gal that I picked up from BYU on campus."

"And where is her body?"

And he said, "I drove out towards Price." He actually told him a little more than that but that was all that was legally given to the press.

This was big news. Bundy was a big deal in Utah, and so when this happened the media in Salt Lake said Bundy confessed to picking up this little gal from BYU and so it was that day, the same day, the phone starts ringing off the hook at the department and the TV channels, Channel 5 and Channel 2 and Channel 4, they all wanted interviews because Bundy had confessed to taking this gal and they heard it the same time we heard it. Big news flash on the TV.

So they came down and interviewed me at the police department, and they said, "What are you going to do?" and I said, "Well, based on what he said and based on what his statements were, we have an idea of where he may of taken her and we are going to go out tomorrow and initiate a search. I made contact with the Carbon County Sheriff and he lined up his sheriff's posse and search and rescue and we will be out there in the morning."

So that morning, some detectives and I head out to Price and we meet the Sheriff. The Sheriff is not in a position to go out there so I said, "Let me take over, sheriff. Look, here is the deal. This is what we are looking for: Bundy said he went through town, within five or six miles of town, and he dumped her. That is all we got. I would have thought by now that a rabbit hunter or deer hunter or somebody would have found the body, so I am not too hopeful, but the media is here and they want to show us searching out through the boonies, so that is what we are going to do."

So, we load up the cars, we get the maps out, and we decide where we are going to go. It isn't where I wanted to go. It isn't where Bundy told us where he dumped her. I didn't want them out there stomping around and destroying evidence. So, we go somewhere else that is a noxious place out in the sagebrush, because those things typically become a circus. You got these deputies and civilians roaming around. We go out in the sagebrush and we divide up into a grid and they start walking and they got metal detectors, and they are finding all sorts of bullets from rabbit hunters and plinkers. They march off on these grids and they are back and forth, back and forth, and I am standing there with the detective that I took and we were just kind of grinning because we know that it is not the place we want to look.

All of a sudden off in the distance from the northeast, a helicopter came flying straight at us and he sits down. There was about six inches of snow on the ground when we were out there in the sagebrush. It was a beautiful day, clear blue sky, and this helicopter sits down and out climbs a camera guy with his tripod and his monster video camera and a CBS reporter from San Francisco that had flown into Denver and chartered a helicopter that cost CBS some money.

So, they split up and interview me standing out there in the sagebrush and I end up on the CBS Evening News with Dan Rather. This clip plays every now and again on some cable show about Bundy. It is still out there.

So, all of that hoopla goes away and the KSL guy, who was a nice guy, was still there. He had been there the whole time and he had seen the interaction with the other detective, and he looked at me and he said, "This is nowhere near where Bundy told you that he dumped her, is it?"

I said, "No it is not."

And he said, "When you go search that area if you find anything would you call me and give us an exclusive?"

And I said, "Yes, and I appreciate you keeping this under your hat." He was a smart guy.

When that is all over with, we bundle up our car, we go back, and I get maps out. Some of the other investigators, maybe from the Northwest, said Bundy had a habit of driving and making a left turn and another left turn. I don't know where that came from but this was kind of his MO as he would dump his bodies. He didn't bury them, he just covered them up a little bit with whatever he could find; and so, based on his comments and based on the maps and the road layout, we had a pretty good idea of where he would go.

He said that he drove out of town 10 miles, made a left on a road, and then made another quick left out in this open area. Well the best spot we could find was kind of a place where people dump stuff, a local dump site, and what better spot to put a body because people are going to go out there and smell something. They would also dump their dead dog or cat or cow or whatever. Think about it, it was the perfect place for him to dispose of the body. Remember she is wearing a long yellow formal dress, so we are thinking a 20-inch zipper on the back of this dress may have survived, and she had a full set of dental appliances. So, we are hoping that maybe the skull or jaw may be found, and we have the metal detector and we are digging and digging, and I find a chuck of zipper with some fabric and sent it up to the crime lab but they couldn't distinguish it, because it was so bleached out that they had no idea of the color, and we couldn't find hide nor hair of the skull. There were all kinds of critters out there that made nests, and coyotes are out there, so who knows? We spent three days out there on our hands and knees, digging through this stuff.

This was probably a week later; it had warmed up and the snow was gone. So, we are pretty much at the end of our rope. And I am standing there...

Let me back up. When the media frenzy was over and they had bugged me and they wanted to know where the mom and dad were living, I wouldn't tell them. I didn't give them phone numbers, I didn't give them anything, because they had moved several times from Bountiful. After that media frenzy day, I called them and they had heard it on the media, on the news, and I said that I was not going to give them their names and numbers, if you want to call them, you can call them, but I am not going to.

We had an idea of where we were going to search. It's out here, and the wife said something very interesting, she said, "You know, when we moved out here four or five years ago, I just had this feeling that she was close."

So, after that second day or third day crawling on our hands and knees, I am standing there, it is done, we have finished, and I am looking back over towards Wellington, and I can almost see the family home where the parents were living. It was really kind of eerie because mom and dad had this feeling that she was close, and I think she was, based on what Bundy had said, how far he said that he drove. If I had been back there, I would have a set of maps and he would have pinpointed the area. So, it was really kind of interesting.

And even after that, any time a body was found I would perk up if I heard female body, human remains anywhere up that direction. I would perk up and wonder, but with decomposition out in the area and the critters, I don't think a body would last very long.

After I left the department, one of my detectives would pull that case file out every couple of years and make a phone call to the mom and dad and say that the file is still here, we haven't forgotten about it, and that we keep looking.

Appendix V

BELOW IS AN IMAGE OF TED'S TWIST

TWIST

Two Word Incomplete Sentences Test

Complete these sentences with one or two words. Try to express your feelings. Try to do every one.

Name TED BUNDY   No. 0522   Sex MALE   Date 4-1-76

1. I feel CHALLENGED   2. My mind is ACTIVE
3. A good way to relax is LISTEN TO MUSIC
4. A person just isn't himself when AFRAID
5. It would be too easy to BE DEPRESSED
6. It's hard to express feelings of PRISON LIFE
7. The only thing that really matters in this world is HAPPINESS AND PEACE
8. Things would be great if I could BE ACQUITTED
9. I've never HURT ANYONE   10. I need FREEDOM
11. I feel I have to KEEP LEARNING
12. A person is most helpless when WITHDRAWN FROM OTHERS
13. My mother was usually LOVING
14. Most people think I am (AM SURE AM) INNOCENT
15. Marriage is INTIMATE PARTNERSHIP   16. I can't STOP STRUGGLING
17. I wish I hadn't COME TO UTAH
18. It's easy to get into trouble when STARS AREN'T CONSIDERED
19. When I was a child I felt CONSTANT ADVENTURE
20. I want to know why ABOUT EVERYTHING
21. I am CONFIDENT   22. Drugs are DESTRUCTIVE
23. Worse than being lonely is being UNLOVED
24. Women are MEN'S EQUALS   25. I hate PREJUDICE
26. When frustrated I DESENSITIZE
27. The thing I remember about my father was BOUNDLESS ENERGY
28. In the future there will be NEW OPPORTUNITIES
29. Compared to most families mine usually WAS CLOSE
30. What excites me is SPRING-TIME
31. I don't like people who are SOLICITOUS
32. I think most girls should BE THEMSELVES
33. My greatest weakness is PROCRASTINATION
34. Some day I will become AN ATTORNEY
35. I wish I could lose the fear of HYPOCRITIC JUDGES
36. I was proud of myself when FINISHED COLLEGE
37. I couldn't live without CERTAIN PEOPLE
38. Tests like this are OBLIGATORY; OBTUSE

Psychological Resources
725 West 120 North
Orem, Utah 84057

Appendix VI

THE DIVIDED SELF

TOWARDS AN UNDERSTANDING OF THE DARK SIDE OF THE SERIAL KILLER
A.L. Carlisle, Ph.D.

"I knew myself, at the first breath of this new life,
to be more wicked, sold a slave to my original evil;
and the thought, in that moment, braced and delighted
me like wine." (The Strange Case of Dr. Jekyll
and Mr.
Hyde by Robert Lewis Stevenson.)

The Jekyll and Hyde story is a fictional account of a person who, through chemical experimentation, becomes transformed into two separate entities, each with his own set of realities, and each having diametrically opposite intentions. Even though it is fiction, this story is often used as a simile to describe opposing the personality states of an offender whose violent acts appear incongruent with the image others have of him. Ted Bundy, Christopher Wilder, and John Wayne Gacy, for example, were each perceived as upstanding citizens, yet each was a vicious killer. Each was intelligent, energetic, and actively involved in the community. Bundy graduated from college, and later went on into law school. He worked on a crisis line in an attempt to help others, and was a field worker in political campaigns. He obtained adequate grades in his law classes even though he was simultaneously killing victims. He is believed to have killed over 30 women.

Wilder was a wealthy co-owner of a construction business, owned Florida real estate worth about a half million dollars, always had plenty of girlfriends, and was liked by those who lived around him. Yet, he killed eight people, torturing many of them. Gacy had a successful business, would dress up like a clown to cheer up sick kids in hospitals, and was a Jaycee "Man of the Year." When the snow became deep, he would hook up a snowplow and clean out the driveways of the homes on his block. Each year, he sponsored a celebration for about 400 people in Chicago at his own expense. And he killed 30-plus victims. Each of these offenders was admired by many, yet each was a serial killer whose dark side was demonstrated by the vicious manner in which a victim's life was taken.

Were they originally good people who went astray or were they born evil and had the ability to hide their sadistic homicidal tendencies from those around them? The evidence accumulated on each would suggest the first postulation to be the accurate one. The pathological process that leads to the development of an obsessive appetite (and possibly an addiction) to kill is still one of the most perplexing psychological mysteries yet to be solved.

Is the Serial Killer Mentally Ill?

While it is tempting to explain the behavior of these killers by labeling them psychotic or insane, psychiatric data usually contradicts such a conclusion. Each of these three, for example, was able to carry out a fairly high level of daily functioning while committing his crimes. Each made logical, and often creative, decisions in his work. Those closest to each of them generally did not see indications of severe mental illness, nor of violent tendencies, and were surprised when the person was arrested for murder. While most serial killers are not insane in the legal sense (that is, they know the difference between right and wrong at the time of the crime), it is commonly accepted that there is some deviant or pathological process occurring within them that is directly related to the commission of multiple homicides.

A second frequently used explanation in the attempt to understand the serial killer is to label him a psychopath, a term which refers to a person who has a clear perception of reality, but seems to lack feelings of guilt, and commits criminal acts for his own immediate gratification, having little regard for the pain and suffering caused by his actions. In other words, a person who has no conscience. While this term may describe the killer's behavior, it still doesn't explain the psychological processes that go on within the person that cause him to kill for pleasure. Nor does it answer the question of whether this lack of conscience resulted in the killing or if psychological pain caused violent tendencies which in turn resulted in suppressing moral promptings. There are many indications that some serial killers experience strong remorse when they kill, at least in the beginning, which shows some capacity to experience guilt. Yet, in spite of the regret for their act, they go on to kill again. Clearly, there have to be some ingredients in the process of the development of the serial killer that have escaped our focus. It is not acceptable any longer to use the terms "monster" or "psychopathic killer" as *explanatory* mechanisms. An increased understanding of the psychological processes that take place within the offender prior to, during, and following the criminal act may help in recognizing and alleviating the problem earlier in the person's life.

While there are many possibilities, one area which has been minimally explored includes the concepts of fantasy, dissociation, and compartmentalization, which results in what many offenders refer to as a dark, sinister, twisted self that hungers for sordid and depraved experiences that would have created deep feelings of revulsion earlier in the killer's life. The purpose of this article is to suggest how this sinister dark side of the person is sparked into existence and develops through common psychological processes. The utility of understanding the process for the mental health profession is in recognizing and redirecting this process in youth. For law enforcement, the utility is towards the development of investigation and interviewing techniques that can enhance the detection and conviction process.

Dissociation and the Separate Self

The concept of an altered self, or altered identity, has its scientific roots in the findings of such persons as Sigmund Freud, Carl Jung, Pierre Janet, and Josef Breuer (see Ellenberger, 1970). Freud postulated that there was a subconscious mind, a "hidden" level of consciousness generally not accessible to the conscious processes. He demonstrated fairly conclusively that traumatic memories and emotions from a person's past could be housed in the subconscious, which could later have a strong effect on the emotional life and behaviors of that person. Freud and Breuer (1957) found a connection between behavioral symptoms and subconscious memories, which they referred to as a "splitting of consciousness" or dual consciousness processes (p.12).

The concept of separate parts or personality types is the basis for Eric Berne's popular *Games People Play* and the field of Transactional Analysis which hypothesizes the interplay of personality structures within each of us called the "child," "adult," and "parent," states. Ernest Hilgard (1977) comments regarding simultaneous, dual levels of thinking:

> Even more intriguing and puzzling is the possibility that in some instances part of the attentive effort and planning [which a person may engage in] may continue without any awareness of it at all. When that appears to be the case, the concealed part of the total ongoing thought and action may be described as *dissociated* from the conscious experience of the person (p. 2).

John and Helen Watkins (1978) have found the presence of "ego states" within many people that are more than simply attitudes or moods, and which are parallel to Hilgard's finding of a Hidden Observer (see Hilgard, 1977). Following up on the findings of Paul Federn, they postulated that these ego states are personality systems which have split off from the main personality. They found these fractionated personality states to be fairly common in many people, to be somewhat independent from each other, and to have a strong controlling effect on the person.

The process of dissociation is a normal psychological process which provides the opportunity for a person to avoid, to one degree or another, the presence of memories and feelings that are too painful to tolerate. Dissociation is a continuum of experiences ranging from the process of blocking out events going on around us (such as when watching a movie) to Dissociative Identity Disorder (DID) where personalities are separate, compartmentalized entities. The ego states referred to by Watkins and Watkins, the Hidden Observer referred to by Hilgard, and the concepts of the entity, dark side, and shadow referred to by various homicide offenders are somewhere between the two extremes. These are sub-DID level states of consciousness that have been created by the person in an attempt to better adapt to his world.

The Role of Fantasy

In the usual case of dissociation, traumatic memories are buried, allowing the person to avoid experiencing the pain. On the opposite side of the coin is the process of creating fantasy, imagery, or illusions, for the purpose of avoiding pain and generating excitement. Walter Young (1988) found that a traumatized child who became DID would incorporate fantasy imagery into a personality identity. In the same manner, a child who experiences excessive emptiness and engages in extensive daydreaming may reach the point where the identity or entity generated through the fantasy becomes a compartmentalized and controlling factor in the person's life.

A fantasy is an imagery process in which a person attempts to obtain vicarious gratification by engaging in acts in his mind which he currently isn't able to do (or doesn't dare do) in reality. Fantasy is a mechanism by which a temperament, such as anger, begins to take on form with a specified purpose and direction. Ongoing and intense fantasy is also a mechanism by which hate and bitterness can begin to become dissociated and compartmentalized from the more ethically focused aspects of the mind. Intensely painful memories and deep emptiness can lead to deep fantasies, which over time take on a greater and greater degree of reality.

When a person is totally absorbed in a fantasy, he dissociates things going on around him. Anger and emptiness become the energy and motivating forces behind the fantasy. While in the fantasy, the person experiences a sense of excitement and relief. However, when it is over, there is still a feeling of emptiness because the fantasy has whetted an appetite for the real thing, which he anticipates will be even more enjoyable than the fantasy. Thus, through fantasy, the person creates a make-believe world wherein he can accomplish what he can't do in reality. Over time, the person may turn to this pseudo-existence with increasing rapidity when he feels stress, depression, or emptiness. This leads to a bifurcated cognitive identity, one being that associated with reality and the people he associates with every day (Carl Jung's Persona) and the other the secret identity which is able to manifest the power and control he would like over others (Carl Jung's Shadow). If the person is angry and bitter, this alter identity often becomes an image of destruction. The major problem is that heavy fantasy is inexorably linked to the process of dissociation and compartmentalization.

As the person shifts back and forth between the two identities in his attempt to meet his various needs, they both become an equal part of him, the opposing force being suppressed when he is attempting to have his needs met through the one. Over time, the dark side (representing the identity or entity the person has created to satisfy his deepest hunger) becomes stronger than the "good" side, and the person begins to experience being possessed, or controlled, by the dark side of him. This is partly because the dark side is the part anticipated to meet the person's strongest needs, and partly because the good side is the part that experiences the guilt over the "evil" thoughts, and therefore out of necessity is routinely suppressed. Thus, the monster is created. Bill[1], who became a multiple homicide offender, describes the need he had for fantasy as a child:

> Without [hero fantasies] I would have had to live with myself. What would have been the alternative? I go out into the garage and I'm in there reading a book or reading one Reader's Digest article after another. If I'm not doing that I'm back inside the house where I'm a nobody. If I'm not doing that, I'm out there on the school yard playing ball, maybe, but still a nobody (personal correspondence).

Bill would become absorbed in the fantasies to the point he had a difficult time living his day-to-day life without them.

Over the years, Bill relied on his fantasy life for his major satisfaction, always still yearning for the fulfilling social life that would replace the fantasies. However, when it didn't come, bitterness and revenge fantasies replaced the hero fantasies. Still wanting to be a socially respected person, Bill attempted to suppress his violent urges while concomitantly relying on his increasingly more violent fantasies to gratify his urges for retribution. This created a serious motivational imbalance in his mental system that resulted in a compartmentalization of the opposing motivational forces (the desire to be a respectable citizen and the opposing desire to get revenge) so that he could have some sense of balance in his life. Ted Bundy described an attempt to keep the two opposing forces separate:

> ... as we've witnessed the development of this darker side of this person's life, we'd expect to see how very closely controlled and separated this part of him

became, and how he was able to keep it, ah, more or less, *from* those around him who thought he was normal. And because this separation was so distinct and well maintained, we would find it unlikely [that] the roles could get confused (p. 195).

However, the roles do begin to get confused, which results in an even greater attempt to keep these identities or forces separate in order to maintain the appearance of normalcy. The process of suppression results in the development of the sinister or dark side of the personality.

The Creation of the Shadow

The vicarious enjoyment of fantasy is enhanced through a self-sustained hypnotic or dissociated "trance," and it creates an appetite which begins to get out of control. Ted Bundy, in telling Michaud and Aynesworth (1989) how a psychopathic killer is created, stated:

> There is some kind of weakness that gives rise to this individual's interest in the kind of sexual activity involving violence that would gradually begin to absorb some of his fantasy... eventually the interest would become so demanding toward new material that it could only be catered to by what he could find in the dirty book stores... (p. 68).

As this process continues, it begins to dominate his life. Bundy continues:

> By peeping in windows, as it were, and watching a woman undress, or watching whatever could be seen, you know, during the evening, and approaching it

almost like a project, throwing himself into it, uh, literally for years he gained, you'd say, a terrific amount of, at times, a great amount of gratification from it and he became increasingly adept at it as anyone becomes adept at anything they do over and over and over again... and as the condition develops and its purposes or characteristics become more well defined, it begins to demand more of the attention and time of the individual, there is a certain amount of tension, uh, struggle between the normal personality and this, this, uh, psychopathological, uh, entity (ibid, p. 70).

Bob[2] a homicide offender, described his experience of the development of this entity, dark side, or shadow within him prior to his homicide:

The beast can take over to complete an identity if you leave a hole in yourself. In other words, it seeks a vacuum. In a healthy person, the vacuum doesn't exist. There's a sense of identity that prevents a need for the dark awareness.
It was very much like there was a battlefield in my head, wrestling with what I as a human being felt to be reasonable alternatives. It was a battle between two very different parts of myself—goodness and evil. When you feel evil, there is a sense of power. It can consume you. There is not much intellect involved in making an evil decision. It's a more gripping thing, more animalistic. It's so much simpler and so much easier to give in to it than to hang on to a moral structure that you don't understand, or an ethic or value or commitment, all the things that make us human being[s] (interview with Bob).

Appendix VI • 237

The offender may attempt to curtail the developing problem:

> I just kept trying to shake it off and physically I would shake my head to rid myself of the thoughts. I wondered where it could come from, or without my pulse going how I could consider such an ugly sequence of events (ibid).
> When this didn't work, he attempted to indulge in the fantasy rather than fight it, to see if that would work. He continued:
> Let's give in to the thoughts. Let's not try to resist it. Let's grovel in it for maybe 20 minutes. Maybe that will dissipate it. Maybe it will blow off some steam. Let's have a fantasy, okay? What happened was I became preoccupied with the fantasy. It did not resolve itself (ibid).

This begins to get more and more out of the person's control, as evidenced by the Boston Strangler:

> I could not stop what I was doing. This thing building up in me—all the time—I knew I was getting out of control (Frank, 1966, p. 326).

Ultimately, when a person has visualized killing over and over again, a time may come when an actual event, similar to what he has been fanaticizing about, presents itself. At such time, under the right circumstances, the offender finds himself automatically carrying out an act he has practiced so many, many times in his mind. Finally, inevitably, this force —this entity—makes a breakthrough. Bundy commented:

> The urge to do something to that person [a woman

he saw] seized him—in a way he'd never been
affected before. And it seized him strongly. And to
the point where, uh, without giving a great deal of
thought, he searched around for some instrumen-
tality to uh, uh, attack this woman with... there was
really no control at this point... (ibid, p. 72-73).

The offender may partially, or completely, dissociate the crime (see Carlisle, 1991). Following the event, the offender's mind returns to the realm of the real world and he often experiences surprise, guilt, and dismay that such an act could have happened. Bundy adds:

What he had done terrified him, purely terrified him.
And he was full of remorse and, you know, he
quickly sobered up, as it were, the sobering effect of
that was to, for some time, close up the cracks again.
And not do anything. For the first time, he sat back
and swore to himself that he wouldn't do something
like that again or even anything that would lead to it.
Within a matter of months, slowly but surely, the
impact of this event lost its, uh, deterrent value. And
within months he was back, uh, uh, peeping in
windows again and slipping back into that old
routine (ibid, p. 74-75).

By acting out the fantasy, the dark side or Shadow now becomes a more permanent part of the person's personality structure. Bundy adds:

Well, we, we ah, described this individual and found
that his behavior, which was becoming more and
more frequent, was also *concomitantly*... occupying
more and more of his mental and intellectual ener-

gies. So, he's facing a greater, ah, more frequent *challenge* of this darker side of himself to his normal life (ibid, p. 171).

Within the offender there is a revulsion of the act, but there is also a sense of excitement, satisfaction, and peace. If the feeling of peace is profound, as if a great load has been taken off the person's shoulders, he is especially likely to become a serial killer. The Shadow becomes stronger because the person has now transcended that final boundary, most inhibitions against killing are gone, and overwhelmingly painful guilt is suppressed. Still, there are some feelings and beliefs against killing. The good side isn't dead, just pushed away. Thus, there is generally a period of time before another homicide occurs.

The offender may begin tempting the Fates a little by allowing himself to engage in some of his earlier pre-homicide activities, thinking this will help satisfy the need that is still growing within him, yet promising himself he will never go as far as he did the last time. However, a time comes when the urge to again feel that power and control becomes so strong the offender gives in to it. Bob describes his experience of the fantasy about the plan to commit homicide:

> My mouth would dry up, my peripheral vision would narrow, and I would be at peace. This was a plan that, whatever [the] cost, [I] would accomplish what I wanted and would create balance in my life. There is a sweetness in surrendering to any plan. To allow yourself to commit to a plan provides a platform in your life where you're not at drift... here there is power. Here there is meaning, logic and order and stability. If I have to give in to an evil thing to do it, it is worth it (interview with Bob).

Another homicide is committed. He may again experience guilt and may again promise to himself that it will never happen again. However, his identity has now drastically changed.

The Obsession

He has become the very being he had so often visualized in his fantasies, even though the possibility of becoming such was so abhorrent to him. He has stepped over the line and cannot step back. The only way he can handle the guilt is to compartmentalize it and thus not consciously experience it. But the guilt doesn't go away. It remains hidden beneath the surface, grinding on the offender, which often produces an eventual deterioration in the killer's personality.

The subsequent homicides are often not as satisfying as the first one was, and do not reach the level of satisfaction of his fantasies. The killer's search for the ultimate high becomes obsessive. Usually by this time, the offender senses the entity within as being a dark side that is very evil and is controlling him, and it terrifies him. He detests it, is fearful of it, yet he basks in its power. He may continue his attempt to fight against its controlling influence, but soon he gives up his struggle against it and allows it to dominate him. His new life becomes a secret existence, usually known only to him.

A drastic identity change has occurred with the opposing identities being farther apart than ever before. Strong self-hate is engendered and, in order to avoid it, the offender has to idealize the pathology. The Shadow has advanced to the level of having become the Controller and is now the dominant force in the offender's life. He can't undo what he has done nor can he face the guilt or accept the responsibility for his behavior. By doing so he would have to face what he has become.

Thus, his sickness becomes his idol and he places himself on a pedestal and worships his own image. For Bill, the two most common traits he experienced at the time of the killings were "... my sense of being perfect and my sense of feeling that I was almost like God" (personal interview). To be divine is to be sinless. To be sinless abnegates blame, and the "evil" act becomes mentally transformed into a divine judgment. The ego dystonic becomes ego syntonic. The offender is hooked. An addiction begins to build, due partly to the attempt to idealize the pathology as a means of avoiding guilt, partly as an attempt to chase the high, and partly in an attempt to find the gratification in reality which the person has found through fantasy.

The offender may begin to flaunt his prowess and feelings of superiority, such as with the Son of Sam (Life-Time Books). He may toy with the police. He savors the knowledge that he is so skillful he can kill people and no one can catch him. He plans, stalks, observes, and executes his crimes with great skill, at times taking great chances because he feels invulnerable. Edmund Kemper, who killed his grandparents, six college-age girls, his mother, and finally his mother's friend, stated:

> It was getting easier to do. I was getting better at it. I started flaunting that invisibility, severing a human head, two of them, at night, in front of my mother's residence, with her at home, my neighbors at home upstairs, their picture window open, the curtain open, eleven o'clock at night, the lights are on. All they had to do was walk by, look out, and I've had it. Some people go crazy at that point. I felt it. It was one helluva tweak (Home Box Office, 1984).

The uncontrollable nature of the urge is expressed by

Charles Hatcher, a serial murderer who began his killing spree in the early 1960s, murdering 13 adults and 3 children. His spree finally ended when he committed himself to a mental hospital the day after he abducted and murdered an 11-year old girl in St. Joseph, Missouri. He admitted to FBI agent Joe Holtslag:

> I kill on impulse. It's an uncontrollable urge that builds and builds over a period of weeks until I have to kill. It doesn't matter if the victims are men, women or children. Whoever is around is in trouble (Ganey, 1989, p. 216-217).

Bob described it this way:

> It was like obeying somebody else. I felt as though I was taking orders and the Shadow was about to say, "No longer will you think of other alternatives."

Regarding the compulsion, Bill stated:

> Once the compulsion is there, it is not a matter of should I or shouldn't I. At this point it's too late. It's a psychological impossibility to stop that activity.

The compulsion is a combination of the planning, the hunt, the capture, the power and control over the victim, the terror she shows, and the possession of the person, often both before and after death.

The excitement combined with the need for companionship and possession is demonstrated in the Dennis Andrew Nilsen and Jeffrey Dahmer cases. Nilsen, a thirty-seven-year old executive officer at the Jobcentre in Kentish Town, London, killed 16 young men; 3 at Cranley Gardens and 13 at his residence in Melrose Avenue. He would invite the victim to his apartment for an evening of companionship and then would kill him. He stated:

> It was intense and all consuming. I needed to do what I did at that time. I had no control over it then. It was a powder keg waiting for a match. I was the match. The kill was only part of the whole. The whole experience which thrilled me intensely was the drink, the chase, the social seduction, the getting the "friend" back, the decision to kill, the body and its disposal.
> The pressure needed release. I took release through spirits and music. On that high I had a loss of morality and danger feeling, if the conditions were right, I would completely follow through to the death. I wished I could stop but I could not. I had no other thrill or happiness (Masters, 1985, p. 241-243).

There may be dissociation during the act as indicated by Albert DeSalvo. Regarding looking in a mirror and seeing himself strangling a Scandinavian woman a week before he killed Anna Slesers, he said:

> I looked in a mirror in the bedroom and there was me—strangling somebody! I fell on my knees and I crossed myself and I prayed, "Oh, God, what am I doing? I'm a married man, I'm the father of two children. God, God, help me!" …. Oh, I got out of there fast. It wasn't like it was me, Mr. Bottomly—it was like it was someone else I was watching (Frank, 1966, p. 313).

Or, dissociation of the event may occur following the

crime as indicated in another of the Boston Strangler's crimes:

> You [meaning himself] was there, these things were going on and the feeling after I got out of that apartment was as if it never happened. I got out and downstairs, and you could have said you saw me upstairs and as far as I was concerned, it wasn't me. I can't explain it to you any other way. It's just so unreal. I was there, it was done, and yet if you talked to me an hour later, or half hour later, it didn't mean nothing, it just didn't mean nothing— (Frank, 1966, p. 320-321).

Habituation, Decline, and Fall

Habituation occurs and the act does not produce the anticipated satisfaction. In an attempt to obtain the level of excitement and fulfillment so desperately sought for, the killer escalates his activities in the form of increased frequency of the crimes and/or increased sadistic acts. Parallel to this there is often a deterioration in the self-image of the offender. He becomes very repulsed by his acts and he begins to hate himself. He feels out of control and helpless in the presence of the Shadow he has created. He feels mastered by his Dark Side. The moralistic part of him fights against the killer within which thirsts for blood. The killer may then reach out for help in some manner. After his eighth victim, the Zodiac Killer of the 1960s wrote a letter to attorney Melvin Belli:

> Dear Melvin, this is the Zodiac speaking
> I wish you a happy Christmass. The one
> thing I ask of you is this,
> please help me. I cannot

> reach out for help because of
> this thing in me won't let me.
> I am finding it extreamly dif-
> icult to hold it in check I am
> afraid I will lose control
> again, and take my ninth &
> posibly tenth victom. Please
> help me I am drownding... (Graysmith, 1987, p. 207).

In another case Bill Heirens wrote a plea for help in red lipstick on a wall of the apartment of his victim just before he killed her:

> For heavens
> Sake catch me
> Before I kill more
> I cannot control myself
> (Freeman, 1956, p. 15)

The overpowering urges to kill pitted against the hate he has developed for himself results in a deterioration in the consistency of his emotions and behavior, and it is more difficult for him to continue to kill as singularly in intent as he has done in the past. He becomes sloppier in his criminal activities, almost as if he were trying to get caught. The Chi Omega killings, for example, were very different from the approach Bundy had used in the past. Arthur Bishop, an offender who sexually molested and killed five boys, began to engage in criminal activities in an attempt to get caught by the police following the fourth homicide. When he got caught following the fifth victim, he fully confessed all of the details of each crime to the police and later said that it was a tremendous relief to get rid of the load he was carrying.

Charles Hatcher voluntarily committed himself to a mental hospital the day after his final homicide and confessed to other killings, partly because another person had been found guilty and had been imprisoned for a crime he had committed.

Following the killing of his first three victims, Wesley Dodd attempted to abduct another victim from a movie theater. The boy fought him off and Dodd narrowly escaped. However, the following week he attempted the same thing in another theater and got caught.

A contract killer I worked with reached the point where he had so much self-hate because of his crimes he ceased to care whether or not he got caught, and he was apprehended easily while committing an amateurish crime. Once the offender has been caught and placed in prison, he may seek psychological counseling out of a need to understand how he developed into the person he became.

While every serial killer does not exactly fit the model suggested here, many do. Finding that a killer has an inner part, or some internal entity, that becomes an overwhelming force in his life and compels him to kill again and again doesn't excuse or justify the person's actions. There is no way to rationalize away a killer's responsibility for his crimes. There may have been some event or events which started the process, but the person himself fed it and allowed it to build and to get out of control. Thus, the person created his own monster, which then controlled him, causing him to do the things he secretly wanted to do in the first place. An understanding of the psychological processes regarding splitting and compartmentalization will aid in the detection process. If this process is not detected and corrected, it continues unabated. The final product is best summarized by a statement Bundy made to the Florida police when they were interrogating him:

I'm the most cold-hearted son of a bitch that you'll ever meet,
(Michaud & Aynesworth, 1983, p. 3)

---

1. Pseudo name
2. Pseudo name

References

Breuer, J. & S. Freud (1957) *Studies on Hysteria*. New York: Basic Books.

Carlisle, A. (1991) Dissociation and Violent Criminal Behavior. Journal of Contemporary Criminal Justice. 7, 273-285.

Damore, L. (1981). *In His Garden: The Anatomy of a Murder*. New York: Dell

Ellenberger, H. (1970). *The Discovery of the Unconscious*. New York: Basic Books.

Frank, G. (1966). *The Boston Strangler*. New York: Signet

Freeman, L. (1956). *Before I Kill More*. New York: Kangaroo Book. p. 15.

Ganey, T. (1989). *Innocent Blood*. New York: St. Martins. p. 216-217.

Graysmith, R. (1987). *Zodiac*. New York: Berkley Books. p. 207.

Hilgard, E. (1977). *Divided Consciousness: Multiple Controls in Human Thought and Action*. New York: John Wiley & Sons.

Home Box Office, American Undercover Series: "Murder, No Apparent Motive" 1984

Jacobi, J. (1973) *The Psychology of C.G. Jung.* New Haven: Yale p. 111

Jung, C. (1983). *Psychiatric Studies. The Collected Works of C.G. Jung.* Vol. 1. New York: Bollingen Series XX/Princeton University Press. p.9.

Masters, B. (1985). *Killing for Company: The Case of Dennis Nilsen.* New York: Stein and Day. p. 241-243.

Michaud, S. & Aynesworth, H. (1983). *The Only Living Witness.* New York: Linden Press/Simon & Schuster.

Michaud, S. & Aynesworth, H. (1989). *Ted Bundy: Conversations with a Killer.* New York: Signet.

Stevenson, R.L. (1963). *Dr. Jekyll and Mr. Hyde.* New York: Scholastic Book Service.

Time-Life Books: Serial Killers. (1992).

Watkins, J. (1978) *The Therapeutic Self.* New York: Human Sciences.

Young, W. Observations on Fantasy in the Formation of Multiple Personality Disorder. *Dissociation*, 1, 13-20.

Acknowledgments

In my first book on Ted, *I'm Not Guilty*, I put in some explanatory findings on how Ted became violent. I believed I understood Ted fairly well because of my testing and interviews with him and my research on violence during my career at the Utah State Prison.

In that first book, I created a mock interview (or what my initial publisher would call a "speculative" interview) between "Ted" and me in which I played both roles in the drama of his life. While the vast majority of the facts mentioned in the "interview" are based on material I had from Ted, from people I interviewed about Ted, or from other violent offenders, some aspects were fill-in speculations to give the "interview" a completeness and continuity. It was because of these occasional speculations that I originally listed that book as a novel.

This raised questions from some readers as to what in that book was speculation and what was accurate.

Steven Booth, my initial publisher, and his wife, Leya Booth, my initial editor, have strongly encouraged me to write books on violence and they suggested I do another book on Ted. This is that book. Carrie Ann Keller, my agent, was also invaluable in keeping me going on this project.

At the time I was beginning my assessment back in the 1970s, there was ample information about what a good guy Ted Bundy was, both when he was arrested and during his trial. Even so, I concluded from my psychological assessment that Ted had a violent personality. In my first book, I put in a number of findings I learned about his personality that allowed me to conclude he was violent. However—and this is the point my then publisher and editor stressed—I didn't tell the reader *how* I had come up with those facts. In other words, I told the reader I was convinced that Ted was violent but I didn't present my justifications for that conclusion.

This book contains the step-by-step process of the psychological assessment I conducted on Ted Bundy. Here, I will explain what I learned about Ted through my evaluation of him that led to my conclusions.

During the time I was conducting this evaluation on Ted, Dr. Alan Roe was a psychologist and close friend of mine who also worked at the Utah State Prison. He helped administer some of the tests and offered his opinions about their results. Dr. Robert Howell and Dr. Reed Payne were consulting psychologists who reviewed my findings and offered their opinions as well. Without their support and efforts, the evaluation wouldn't have been as accurate or compelling, for me or the court.

Shelley Welsh from Nova Scotia offered her time to read the manuscript. Her insight and understanding of Ted were invaluable.

Periodically, I question whether or not the information I present on Ted and other serial killers will be of any use to history. I want to thank the many friends, family, and colleagues who have encouraged me not to give up these projects. Special recognition needs to be given to the late Richard "Dick" Larsen who was an Associate Editor of the Seattle Times when Ted was committing his crimes in Washington. He wrote a book called *The Deliberate Stranger*. I sincerely appreciate his widow, Virginia Larsen, who allowed me access to Dick's research material on Ted.

Most of all, I want to thank the people I called when I was doing my assessment of Ted Bundy. The conclusions I put in my report for Judge Stewart Hansen Jr. primarily come from the information they gave me.

In hindsight looking back on all of this, the most perplexing question may not be what we can learn by studying Ted Bundy, but what we can learn about ourselves. Was he born with a potential for violence or did he develop it over time? And, if he developed it over time, what caused it to go the way it did? Could he have made a change in the direction his life was going and not have ever killed anyone? If Ted had never killed anyone, he likely could have been a popular political figure today.

But I'm getting ahead of my story. My task in the spring of 1976 was to try to understand Ted and to give the court my opinion of his personality.

- Al Carlisle

My conclusions about Ted Bundy are my own. I accept full responsibility for any errors I might have made in this book. AC

Note: Dr. Carlisle passed away in 2018. His literary executor wishes to thank Genius Publishing for their help keeping this book in print, and for working with us as we made the transition to Carlisle Legacy Books, LLC.

This book is based on notes, interviews, and evaluations from 1976. It is true to the best of Dr. Carlisle's recollection.

C. Lindsay Carlisle thanks Janet Summers for giving a second look at the cover design and helping find the right hex colors.

About the Author

Much of Al Carlisle's career dealing with serial killers was as a psychologist at the Utah State Prison from which he retired as the head of the Psychology Department in 1989. He continued to interview serial killers. He wanted to learn why good people chose to do bad things.

Dr. Carlisle performed the first psychological assessment of Ted Bundy in 1976 while he was being held for a 90-day evaluation at the Utah State Prison.

Dr. Carlisle was also a consultant for the Salt Lake Rape Crisis Center for several years and hosted workshops on serial homicide and other crime topics. He conducted extensive research on serial killers and interviewed the Hi Fi killers, Arthur Gary Bishop, Westley Allan Dodd, Keith Jesperson, Ted Bundy and many others.

His specialties include Dissociative Identity Disorder (Multiple Personality Disorder).

Al Carlisle, born and raised in Utah, received a BS and MS from Utah State University and his Ph.D. in clinical psychology from Brigham Young University.

He is the author of five books in the *Development of the Violent Mind* series:

"I'm Not Guilty!" The Case of Ted Bundy

Mind of the Devil: The Cases of Arthur Gary Bishop & Westley Allan Dodd

Broken Samurai: One Marine's Journey from Hero to Hitman

The 1976 Psychological Assessment of Ted Bundy
The Ted Bundy Files: A 1976 Companion

Dr. Carlisle passed away in 2018 at the age of 81.
https://www.alcarlisle.com

Also by Al Carlisle, PhD

Books in the *Development of the Violent Mind* series:

1: *"I'm Not Guilty!" The Case of Ted Bundy*

2: *Mind of the Devil: The Cases of Arthur Gary Bishop & Westley Allan Dodd*

3: *Broken Samurai: One Marine's Journey from Hero to Hitman*

4: *The 1976 Psychological Assessment of Ted Bundy*

5: *The Ted Bundy Files: A 1976 Companion*

Publisher's Note

When Dr. Carlisle passed away in May of 2018, I took over his literary estate. Al's agent, Carrie Anne, and I worked closely to preserve his legacy and to share his 50 years of research into the development of the violent mind.

Dr. Carlisle sought to learn what made good people do bad things. He wanted to help protect kids from becoming victims of predators, or becoming predators themselves. Each of Dr. Carlisle's books has endeavored to help others learn how a person develops into a serial killer. Because if we can learn to recognize a pattern, we may be able to help break it before an irrevocable step is taken.

There is good and evil in each one of us. To quote Professor Dumbledore, "It is our choices…that show what we truly are, far more than our abilities." The same can be said about choosing to act on thoughts and desires that we know are wrong. The people in Dr. Carlisle's books began as basically good, but they made choices that led them, step-by-step down a path to prison.

Dr. Carlisle had a way of looking at the world, and people, that can help all of us gain understanding, and help us want to make better choices. We hope you enjoy this book.

We could not have done this without the invaluable assistance of Steve and Dave.

Charlene & Carrie Anne
   Two blind ladies with cats.

Quote from *Harry Potter and the Chamber of Secrets* by J. K. Rowling

www.ingramcontent.com/pod-product-compliance
Lightning Source LLC
Chambersburg PA
CBHW051533020426
42333CB00016B/1907